DATE DUE

PRINTED IN U.S.A.

RENEWABLE
AND ALTERNATIVE
ENERGY

ENERGY: PAST, PRESENT, AND FUTURE

RENEWABLE AND ALTERNATIVE ENERGY

EDITED BY ROBERT CURLEY, MANAGER, SCIENCE AND TECHNOLOGY

Britannica
Educational Publishing

IN ASSOCIATION WITH

ROSEN
EDUCATIONAL SERVICES

Published in 2012 by Britannica Educational Publishing
(a trademark of Encyclopædia Britannica, Inc.)
in association with Rosen Educational Services, LLC
29 East 21st Street, New York, NY 10010.

First Edition

Britannica Educational Publishing
Michael I. Levy: Executive Editor
J.E. Luebering: Senior Manager
Marilyn L. Barton: Senior Coordinator, Production Control
Steven Bosco: Director, Editorial Technologies
Lisa S. Braucher: Senior Producer and Data Editor
Yvette Charboneau: Senior Copy Editor
Kathy Nakamura: Manager, Media Acquisition
Robert Curley: Manager, Science and Technology

Rosen Educational Services
Jeanne Nagle: Senior Editor
Nelson Sá: Art Director
Cindy Reiman: Photography Manager
Matthew Cauli: Designer, Cover Design
Introduction by Laura Loria

Library of Congress Cataloging-in-Publication Data

Renewable and alternative energy / edited by Robert Curley. — 1st ed.
    p. cm. — (Energy: past, present, and future)
"In association with Britannica Educational Publishing, Rosen Educational Services."
Includes bibliographical references and index.
ISBN 978-1-61530-488-2 (library binding)
1. Renewable energy sources. I. Curley, Robert, 1955-
TJ808.R415 2012
621.042—dc22

                                                    2010044433

Manufactured in the United States of America

On the cover (top, back): A line of offshore turbines. *Shutterstock.com*
Cover (bottom): multiple solar panels catching rays. *Shutterstock.com*

On page viii: Proponents of alternative energy pose in front of solar panels, wearing sun head-dresses, during a Greenpeace event in Quezon City, Philippines. *Jay Directo/AFP/Getty Images*

On pages 1, 17, 29, 52, 67, 75, 84, 100, 115, 117, 119: Wind turbines spin at sunset in Roedgen near Bitterfeld, Germany. *Andreas Rentz/Getty Images*

Contents

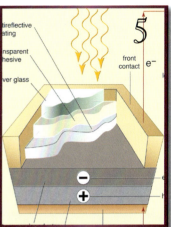

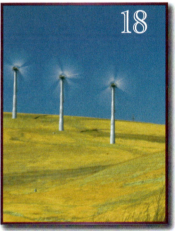

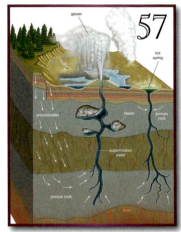

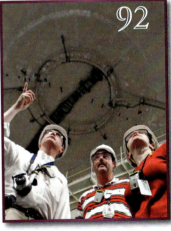

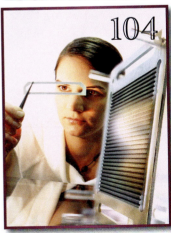

INTRODUCTION

Technology is a dominant force in the world today. Accordingly, the demand for energy to power the various devices that make the world run more smoothly and efficiently has increased at an astonishing rate; world population growth and the modernization of developing nations have strained the availability of some energy resources even further. It has been estimated that 80 percent of global energy comes from fossil fuels such as coal, oil, and natural gas. These limited commodities may soon be depleted if this pattern of usage continues. In addition to scarcity, pollution and other compelling factors suggest that fossil fuels are less than ideal energy sources.

Short of giving up modern conveniences, the answer to this worldwide energy crisis arguably lies in renewable resources, meaning those capable of consistent regeneration, with unlimited potential availability. Several of these renewable resources, collectively termed "alternative energy," are being researched and implemented across the globe. Energy derived from the Sun, wind, water, and heat from Earth's core has been used alongside, or in place of, fossil fuels increasingly over the last century. Biofuels, derived from crops such as corn and sugar cane, and nuclear energy are other alternatives that are receiving a lot of attention of late. This book examines these various alternative energy options—their root sources or creation methods, their applications, and the technology that makes them viable energy resources.

The power of the Sun has been used throughout history. In some ways, it is easy to take advantage of solar energy, from the simple act of hanging clothing to dry on a fair day to placing houseplants near south-facing windows, which receive the most sunlight. Converting that energy into an inexpensive and readily accessible form of power is a bit more complicated. The conversion of solar energy into electricity requires a few more steps, as well as some carefully crafted hardware.

The most common device to harness the Sun's power is called a flat-plate collector. Many people are familiar with a typical flat-plate collector known as a solar panel, which is composed of a black silicon sheet encased in glass. The panel contains a small group of solar cells that convert light into electricity through the photovoltaic effect, which is the reaction caused by light falling on two dissimilar materials. The energy derived from this process can then be used immediately or stored.

Single solar panels are generally found on homes or individual buildings. A larger grouping of solar panels, known as an array, produces electricity that is intended for wide distribution, rather than individual use. While it is renewable and efficient, solar energy also requires an enormous initial monetary investment, from both the individual and public-consumption standpoint.

Wind power has a long history of use as a power source. The first windmills were capture devices wherein a circle of sails, typically arranged on a horizontal axis set atop a tower, were rotated by the wind. The ensuing mechanical energy was used to grind grain and pump water from wells. Advances in windmill technology have included the creation of a hollow tower, inside of which were gears used to power pumps, and the addition of a fantail, which allowed the sails to turn into the wind automatically.

Modern wind turbines retain the same basic design of windmills, incorporating the horizontal axis and a vertical tower, although blades, measuring up to 130 feet long, have replaced sails. Rather than grind grain, the kinetic energy of the wind nowadays is generally converted to electrical energy. Individual turbines can be used to power a home, while groupings of them known as "wind farms" can, theoretically, generate enough energy to supply a small town.

In order to function efficiently, turbines must be located in an area determined to have a wind power rating of at least 3, on a scale of 1 to 7. In the United States, the Great Plains, including Texas, a large producer of wind power, and island locales are best suited for the task.

Despite its simplicity and abundance, the use of wind power continues to receive mixed reviews. Opponents point to modern turbines' aesthetic disadvantages and the potential harm to wildlife; there have been several reports of bird strikes. Also, wind power is not always available close to large population centres.

Considered the world's first machines, waterwheels operate on the same basic principle as a windmill, only the former uses the kinetic energy of falling or flowing water to generate power. Traditional waterwheels had vanes or paddles that were partially submerged into flowing water, causing the wheel to rotate. A shaft connected to the wheel used kinetic energy from the rotating paddles to grind grain, activate saw blades in lumber mills, and operate any number of additional mechanical devices.

During the 19th century, waterwheels were largely replaced by more sophisticated turbines. Today, hydropower is harnessed for public consumption in many parts of the world. Hydropower can be harnessed from the ocean, using tides and waves to propel turbines. This power is sent to transformers, which increase the voltage so that the power can travel to where it is needed. However, hydroelectric power is the most commonly used form of hydropower in use today.

Hydroelectric power is primarily generated through the use of dams or, less frequently, via naturally cascading waterfalls. (For instance, a large percentage of electricity in New York State is generated by currents created by Niagara Falls.) The basic procedure for gathering power involves collecting water from a higher elevation and directing it downward. The difference between the elevations of the two points is referred to as the head. A larger head can produce more power. The falling water rotates the multiple turbines, which drive a generator, thus converting the mechanical energy of the falling water into electricity.

The two most common types of turbines used in hydropower collection are impulse turbines and reaction turbines. Impulse turbines direct the water into a narrow tube, which shoots the water through a specially designed nozzle into a vessel that extracts the energy. Reaction turbines work by increasing the flow of the water while dropping its pressure, similar to a rotating lawn sprinkler. Other turbine designs are used as well, depending on conditions.

No matter how it is collected, hydropower is both renewable and nonpolluting. Its main drawback lies in its availability. Flowing water is not available everywhere, and long-distance transportation costs are expensive.

An enormous source of heat energy lies beneath Earth's surface. Heat from the interior of our planet is called geothermal energy. Hot springs are one type of natural release for this energy. The resort town of Hot Springs, Arkansas, boasts water that reaches temperatures of 62 °C (143 °F) and higher. Geysers are a more forceful release of geothermal energy. The term "geyser" is derived from the Icelandic word *geysir*, meaning "to gush." Approximately 800 geysers are known to exist in the world. Five hundred of these are located in Yellowstone National Park, including Old Faithful, which spouts an average of every 90 minutes.

While plentiful, underground heat energy is difficult to extract. The heat is created by magma, or molten rock, which raises the temperature of underground water until it is converted to steam. Steam spreads as it rises, like vapour escaping from a teakettle's spout. As it spreads, its kinetic energy decreases. Therefore, it is critical that pockets of geothermal heat be concentrated in order for energy to be collected and utilized. The goal of a steam turbine is to collect the maximum amount of energy possible while reducing turbulence, leakage, and friction. Blade design and turbine staging can control the rate at which steam expands. Geothermal power stations operate in several countries, including Japan, Mexico, Italy, and the United States.

There has been a massive media focus on biofuels in the U.S. early in the 21st century. Biofuels, which provide energy derived from plant or animal waste, are considered cost-effective and eco-friendly, given the abundance and renewability of their sources. Types of biofuels include wood, which can be burned for heat or converted to electricity, methane gas derived from decomposition of organic materials, and liquid fuels, including ethanol and biodiesel, which are distilled from plants.

This energy source is not without its drawbacks. The energy required to produce biofuels such as ethanol detracts significantly from their overall efficiency. Production of these fuels does create pollution, and land diverted to growing biofuel crops—primarily corn and sugar cane—reduces the availability of space to grow food crops. The United States and the European Union have created laws mandating certain levels of biofuel use, but requirements are subject to change in light of new findings.

Alternative fuels also play a role in the advancement of electrochemical energy. Hydrogen-based fuel mixing with oxygen sparks a chemical reaction that produces electricity within fuel cells, which are a longer-lived and cleaner version of batteries. Fuel cells have been used in space exploration for years. Refining the model so that they have practical application on Earth has been a source of great exploration and experimentation, revolving primarily around the automobile industry and companies that produce various types of electrical machinery.

Nuclear energy also is a controversial energy source. Proponents of nuclear energy argue that it is safe, efficient, and clean, while opponents are wary of the potential harm to human life that can occur during a malfunction. Created by a chain reaction of splitting atoms, a process known as fission, nuclear energy is highly complicated and demands precision and attention to safety. Failure to control or contain these materials can result in illness and fatalities for those working at and living near a nuclear power plant. A 1979 accident, largely due to human error, at the Three Mile Island power station in Pennsylvania triggered a near halt to nuclear energy production in the United States.

The core of a nuclear reactor, which is where fission occurs, contains fuel, coolants, moderators, absorbers, reflectors, and controls, which work together to maintain an efficient balance by redirecting atoms while providing stability. The materials used in nuclear fuels include forms of uranium and thorium. Energy is obtained by creating a steady level of fission, referred to as the critical level. Criticality is maintained through the use of absorbers and the careful monitoring of fuel levels. Fission releases heat energy, which can then be converted to electrical energy.

Containment systems, which include fuel cladding, shielding, and nearly airtight structures of concrete, are designed to provide multiple layers of protection against radioactive leakage. Failure to properly contain radioactivity can have devastating results. The former Soviet Union did not require the Chernobyl power stations, located in Ukraine, to have an external containment structure. An explosion at a plant there in 1986 spread more radioactivity than did either of the two atomic bombs dropped on Japan during World War II.

The truth of the matter is that all sources of energy, whether traditional or alternative, have positive and negative aspects. In a society that is increasingly environmentally aware, however, alternative energy is considered the most likely answer to saving our planet's resources for future generations. Experimentation and research of new technologies, which require significant innovation and investment, are expected to increase the overall efficiency of renewable and alternative sources of energy.

CHAPTER 1
CATCHING RAYS:
SOLAR ENERGY

T he Sun is an extremely powerful energy source. Radiation from the Sun is capable of producing heat, causing chemical reactions, and generating electricity. Sunlight is by far the largest source of energy received by the Earth, but its intensity at the Earth's surface is actually quite low. This is essentially because of the enormous radial spreading of radiation from the distant Sun. A relatively minor additional loss is due to the Earth's atmosphere and clouds, which absorb or scatter as much as 54 percent of the incoming sunlight.

Even so, the total amount of solar energy incident on Earth is vastly in excess of the world's current and anticipated energy requirements. If suitably harnessed, this highly diffused source has the potential to satisfy all future energy needs. In the 21st century solar energy is expected to become increasingly attractive as an energy source because of its inexhaustible supply and its nonpolluting character, in stark contrast to the finite fossil fuels coal, petroleum, and natural gas.

SOLAR HEATING

The sunlight that reaches the ground consists of nearly 50 percent visible light, 45 percent infrared radiation, and smaller amounts of ultraviolet and other forms of electromagnetic radiation. This radiation can be converted into thermal energy to heat either water or air in buildings.

There are two types of solar heating: passive and active. Passive heating relies on architectural design to heat buildings. The building's site, structure, and materials can all be utilized to maximize the heating (and lighting) effect of the sunlight falling on it, thereby lowering or even eliminating its fuel requirement. A well-insulated building with a large glass window facing south, for instance, can effectively trap heat on sunny days and reduce reliance on gas or oil (for heating) or electricity (for lighting). Entering sunlight warms the air and the solid surfaces in those rooms exposed to it, and this warmth is carried to other rooms in the building by natural convection. Interior finishes such as brick or tile are often incorporated into buildings to absorb the sunlight and reradiate the heat at night.

In active heating, mechanical means are used to store, collect, and distribute solar energy in buildings in order to provide hot water or space heating. Two main types of devices are used to capture solar energy and convert it to thermal energy: flat-plate collectors and concentrating collectors. Because the intensity of solar radiation at the Earth's surface is so low, both types of collectors must be large in area. Even in sunny parts of the world's temperate regions, for instance, a collector must have a surface area of about 40 square metres (430 square feet) to gather enough energy to serve the energy needs of one person.

The most widely used flat-plate collectors consist of a blackened metal plate, covered with one or two sheets of glass, that is heated by the sunlight falling on it. The glass allows visible light to fall on the plate but traps the resulting heat, which is then transferred to a carrier fluid (usually a liquid, less commonly air) that flows past the back of the plate. The heat may be used directly, or it may be transferred to another medium for storage. Flat-plate collectors typically heat carrier fluids to temperatures ranging from 66 to 93 °C (150 to 200 °F). The efficiency of such collectors (i.e., the proportion of the energy received that they convert into usable energy) ranges from 20 to 80 percent, depending on the design of the collector.

Flat-plate collectors are commonly used for hot-water heating and house heating. The storage of heat for use at night or on cloudy days is commonly accomplished by using insulated tanks to store the water heated during sunny periods. Such a system can supply a home with hot water drawn from the storage tank, or, with the warmed water flowing through tubes in floors and ceilings, it can provide space heating. If the carrier fluid contains anti-freeze to keep it from freezing during cold weather, a heat exchanger is used to transfer the carrier fluid's heat to water that can be used for domestic purposes.

When higher temperatures are needed, a concentrating, or focusing, collector is used. These devices concentrate sunlight received from a wide area onto a small blackened receiver, thereby considerably increasing the light's intensity in order to produce high temperatures. The arrays of carefully aligned mirrors or lenses used in these so-called solar furnaces can focus enough sunlight to heat a target to temperatures of 2,000 °C (3,600 °F) or more.

This heat can be used to study the properties of materials at high temperatures, or it can be used to operate a boiler, which in turn generates steam for a steam-turbine–electric-generator power plant. The solar furnace has become an important tool in high-temperature research. For producing steam, the movable mirrors are so arranged as to concentrate large amounts of solar radiation upon blackened pipes through which water is circulated and thereby heated.

SOLAR POWER

Solar radiation may be converted directly into electricity by solar cells (photovoltaic cells). In such cells, a small electric voltage is generated when light strikes the junction between a metal and a semiconductor (such as silicon) or the junction between two different semiconductors. In the latter case, when sunlight strikes a solar cell, an electron is freed by the photoelectric effect. The two dissimilar semiconductors possess a natural difference in electric potential (voltage), which causes the electrons to flow through the external circuit, supplying power to the load. The flow of electricity results from the characteristics of the semiconductors and is powered entirely by light striking the cell.

Unfortunately, though solar energy itself is free, the high cost of its collection, conversion, and storage still limits its exploitation. The energy efficiency of most present-day photovoltaic cells is only about 15 to 20 percent, and since the intensity of solar radiation is low to begin with, huge and costly assemblies of cells such as the arrays at Olmedilla are required to produce electric power on a municipal scale. Consequently, photovoltaic cells that operate on sunlight or artificial light have so far found major commercial use only in low-power applications—as power sources for calculators and watches, for example. Larger units have been used to provide power for water pumps and communications systems in remote areas and for weather and communications satellites.

Nevertheless, the potential for solar power is enormous, since about 200,000 times the world's total daily electric-generating capacity is received by the Earth every day in the form of solar energy. While total photovoltaic energy production is minuscule, it is likely to increase as fossil fuel resources shrink. In fact, the world's current energy consumption could be supplied by covering less than 1 percent of the Earth's surface with solar panels. The material requirements would be enormous but feasible, as silicon is the second most abundant element in the

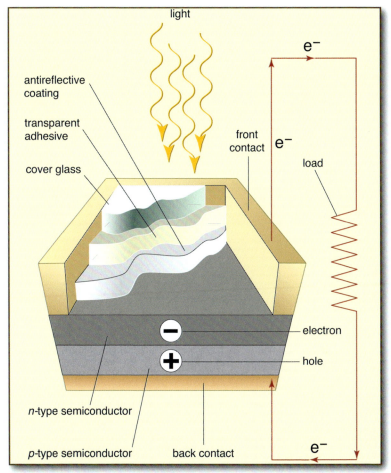

light

antireflective
coating

transparent
adhesive

cover glass

front
contact

load

e⁻

e⁻

e⁻

electron

hole

n-type semiconductor

p-type semiconductor   back contact

Diagram of a solar cell with different semiconductors converting sunlight to electricity. © Merriam-Webster Inc.

Earth's crust. These factors have led solar proponents to envision a future "solar economy" in which practically all of humanity's energy requirements are satisfied by cheap, clean, renewable sunlight.

SOLAR CELLS AND SOLAR PANELS

Technically, a solar cell, or photovoltaic cell, is any device that directly converts the energy in light into electrical energy through the photovoltaic effect. The overwhelming majority of solar cells are fabricated from silicon—with increasing efficiency and lowering cost as the materials range from amorphous (noncrystalline) to polycrystalline to crystalline (single crystal) silicon forms. Unlike batteries or fuel cells, solar cells do not utilize chemical reactions or require fuel to produce electric power. Unlike electric generators, they do not have any moving parts.

THE PHOTOVOLTAIC EFFECT

When two dissimilar materials in close contact produce an electrical voltage when struck by light or other radiant energy, they are demonstrating the photovoltaic effect. For instance, when light strikes crystals such as silicon or germanium, in which electrons are usually not free to move from atom to atom within the crystal, it provides the energy needed to free some electrons from their bound condition. Free electrons cross the junction between two dissimilar crystals more easily in one direction than in the other, giving one side of the junction a negative charge and, therefore, a negative voltage with respect to the other side, just as one electrode of a battery has a negative voltage with respect to the other.

The photovoltaic effect can continue to provide voltage and current as long as light continues to fall on the two materials. This current can be used to measure the brightness of the incident light or as a source of power in an electrical circuit, as in a solar power system.

The photovoltaic effect in a solar cell can be illustrated with an analogy to a child on a slide. Initially, both the electron and the child are in their respective "ground states." Next, the electron is lifted up to its excited state by consuming energy received from the incoming light, just as the child is lifted up to an "excited state" at the top of the slide by consuming chemical energy stored in his body. In both cases there is now energy available in the excited state that can be expended.

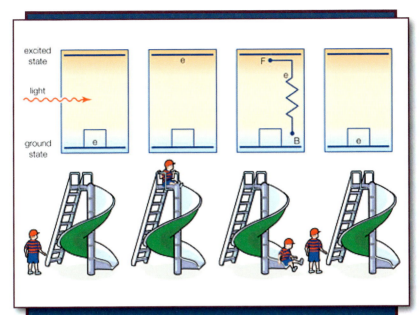

Representation of an electron in a solar cell. Encyclopaedia Britannica, Inc.

In the absence of junction-forming materials, there is no incentive for excited, free electrons to move along a specific direction; they eventually fall back to the ground state. On the other hand, whenever two different materials are placed in contact, an electric field is generated along the contact. This is the so-called built-in field, and it exerts a force on free electrons, effectively "tilting" the electron states and forcing the excited free electrons into an external electrical load where their excess energy can be dissipated. The external load can be a simple resistor, or it can be any of myriad electrical or electronic devices ranging from motors to radios. Correspondingly, the child moves to the slide because of his desire for excitement. It is on the slide that the child dissipates his excess energy.

Finally, when the excess energy is expended, both the electron and the child are back in the ground state, where they can begin the whole process over again. The motion of the electron, like that of the child, is in one direction. In short, the photovoltaic effect produces a direct current (DC)—one that flows constantly in only a single direction.

The power generated by a single photovoltaic cell is typically only about 2 watts. However, solar cells can be arranged into large groupings called arrays. These arrays, composed of many thousands of individual cells, can function as central electric power stations, converting sunlight into electrical energy for distribution to industrial, commercial, and residential users. By connecting large numbers of individual cells together in solar-panel arrays, hundreds of thousands, or even millions, of watts of electric power can be generated in a solar electric plant. For example, the Olmedilla Photovoltaic Power Park in Olmedilla de Alarcón, Spain, the world's largest installed solar power plant upon its completion in 2008, links together more than 160,000 solar panels to generate as much as 60 megawatts (60 million watts) of electricity. Other solar power plants are in the works to generate hundreds of megawatts of electricity.

Solar cells in much smaller configurations, commonly referred to as solar cell panels or simply solar panels, have been installed by homeowners on their rooftops to replace or augment their conventional electric supply. Solar cell panels also are used to provide electric power in many remote terrestrial locations where conventional electric power sources are either unavailable or prohibitively expensive to install.

Because they have no moving parts that could need maintenance or fuels that would require replenishment, solar cells provide power for most space installations, from communications and weather satellites to space stations. (Solar power is insufficient for space probes sent to the outer planets of the solar system or into interstellar space, however, because of the diffusion of radiant energy with distance from the Sun.) Another application of solar cells is in consumer products, such as electronic toys, handheld calculators, and portable radios. Solar cells used in devices of this kind may utilize artificial light (e.g., from incandescent and fluorescent lamps) as well as sunlight.

SOLAR CELL STRUCTURE AND OPERATION

Whether they are used in a central power station, a satellite, or a calculator, solar cells have the same basic structure. Light enters the device through an optical coating, or antireflection layer, that minimizes the loss of light by reflection, effectively trapping the light that falls on the solar cell by promoting its transmission to the energy-conversion layers below. The antireflection layer is typically an oxide of silicon, tantalum, or titanium that is formed on the cell surface by spin-coating or a vacuum deposition technique.

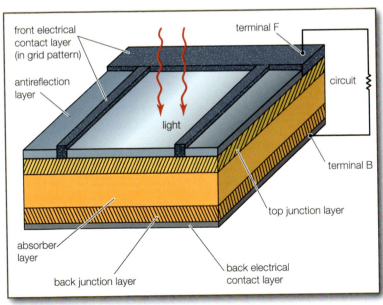

A commonly used solar cell structure. In many such cells, the absorber layer and the back junction layer are both made of the same material. Encyclopædia Britannica, Inc.

The three energy-conversion layers below the antire-flection layer are the top junction layer; the absorber layer, which constitutes the core of the device; and the back junction layer. Two additional electrical contact layers are needed to carry the electric current out to an external load and back into the cell, thus completing an electric circuit. The electrical contact layer on the face of the cell where light enters is generally present in some grid pattern and is composed of a good conductor such as a metal. Since metal blocks light, the grid lines are as thin and widely spaced as is possible without impairing collection of the current produced by the cell. The back electrical contact layer has no such diametrically opposed restrictions. It need simply function as an electrical contact and thus covers the entire back surface of the cell structure. Because the back layer also must be a very good electrical conductor, it is always made of metal.

Since most of the energy in sunlight and artificial light is in the visible range of electromagnetic radiation, a solar cell absorber should be efficient in absorbing radiation at those wavelengths. Materials that strongly absorb visible radiation belong to a class of substances known as semiconductors; those that are about one-hundredth of a centimetre thick or less can absorb all incident visible light. Since the junction-forming and contact layers are much thinner, the thickness of a solar cell is essentially that of the absorber. Examples of semiconductor materials employed in solar cells include silicon, gallium arsenide, indium phosphide, and copper indium selenide.

When light falls on a solar cell, electrons in the absorber layer are excited from a lower-energy "ground state," in which they are bound to specific atoms in the solid, to a higher "excited state," in which they can move through the solid. In the absence of the junction-forming layers, these "free" electrons are in random motion, and so there can be no oriented direct current. The addition of junction-forming layers, however, induces a built-in electric field that produces the photovoltaic effect. In effect, the electric field gives a collective motion to the electrons that flow past the electrical contact layers into an external circuit where they can do useful work.

The materials used for the two junction-forming layers must be dissimilar to the absorber in order to produce the built-in electric field and to carry the electric current. Hence, these may be different semiconductors (or the same semiconductor with different types of conduction), or they may be a metal and a semiconductor. The materials used to construct the various layers of solar cells are essentially the same as those used to produce the diodes and transistors of solid-state electronics and microelectronics. Solar cells and microelectronic devices share the same basic technology. In solar cell fabrication, however, one seeks to construct a large-area device because the power produced is proportional to the illuminated area. In microelectronics the goal is, of course, to construct electronic components of ever smaller dimensions in order to increase their density and operating speed within semiconductor chips, or integrated circuits.

Since solar cells obviously cannot produce electric power in the dark, part of the energy they develop under light is stored, in many applications, for use when light is not available. One common means of storing this electrical energy is by charging electrochemical storage batteries. This sequence of converting the energy in light into the energy of excited electrons and then into stored chemical energy is strikingly similar to the process of photosynthesis, the process by which the energy in light is converted into chemical energy in plants.

SOLAR PANEL DESIGN

Most solar cells are a few square centimetres in area and protected from the environment by a thin coating of glass or transparent plastic. Because a typical 10 cm × 10 cm (4 inch × 4 inch) solar cell generates only about two watts of electrical power (15 to 20 percent of the energy of light incident on their surface), cells are usually combined in series to boost the voltage or in parallel to increase the current. A solar, or photovoltaic (PV), module generally consists of 36 interconnected cells laminated to glass within an aluminum frame. In turn, one or more of these modules may be wired and framed together to form a solar panel.

Solar panels are slightly less efficient at energy conversion per surface area than individual cells because of inevitable inactive areas in the assembly and cell-to-cell variations in performance. The back of each solar panel is equipped with standardized sockets so that its output can be combined with other solar panels to form a solar array. A complete photovoltaic system may consist of many solar panels, a power system for accommodating different electrical loads, an external circuit, and storage batteries. Photovoltaic systems are broadly classifiable as either stand-alone or grid-connected systems.

Stand-alone systems contain a solar array and a bank of batteries directly wired to an application or load circuit. A battery system is essential to compensate for the absence of any electrical output from the cells at night or in overcast conditions, adding considerably to the overall cost. Each battery stores direct current (DC) electricity at a fixed voltage determined by the panel specifications, although load requirements may differ. DC-to-DC converters are used to provide the voltage levels demanded by DC loads, and DC-to-AC inverters supply power to alternating current (AC) loads. Stand-alone systems are ideally suited for remote installations where linking to a central power station is prohibitively expensive. Examples include pumping water for feedstock and providing electric power to lighthouses, telecommunications repeater stations, and mountain lodges.

Grid-connected systems integrate solar arrays with public utility power grids in two ways. One-way systems are used by utilities to supplement power grids during midday peak usage. Bidirectional systems are used by companies and individuals to supply some or all of their power needs, with any excess power fed back into a utility power grid. A major advantage of grid-connected systems is that no storage batteries are needed. The corresponding reduction in capital and maintenance costs is offset, however, by the increased complexity of the system. Inverters and additional protective gear are needed to interface low-voltage DC output from the solar array with a high-voltage AC power grid. Additionally, rate structures for reverse

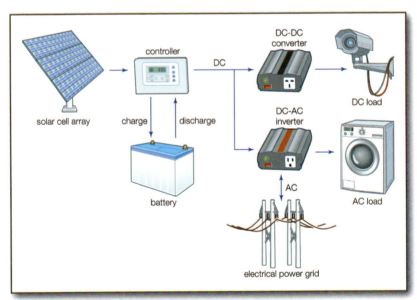

A grid-connected solar cell system. Encyclopædia Britannica, Inc.

metering are necessary when residential and industrial solar systems feed energy back into a utility grid.

The simplest deployment of solar panels is on a tilted support frame or rack known as a fixed mount. For maximum efficiency, a fixed mount should face south in the Northern Hemisphere or north in the Southern Hemisphere, and it should have a tilt angle from horizontal of about 15 degrees less than the local latitude in summer and 25 degrees more than the local latitude in winter. More complicated deployments involve motor-driven tracking systems that continually reorient the panels to follow the daily and seasonal movements of the Sun. Such systems are justified only for large-scale utility generation using high-efficiency concentrator solar cells with lenses or parabolic mirrors that can intensify solar radiation a hundredfold or more.

Although sunlight is free, the cost of materials and available space must be considered in designing a solar system. Less-efficient solar panels imply more panels, occupying more space, in order to produce the same amount of electricity. Compromises between cost of materials and efficiency are particularly evident for space-based solar systems. Panels used on satellites have to be extra-rugged, reliable, and resistant to radiation damage encountered in the Earth's upper atmosphere. In addition, minimizing the liftoff weight of these panels is more critical than fabrication costs.

Another factor in solar panel design is the ability to fabricate cells in "thin-film" form on a variety of substrates, such as glass, ceramic, and plastic, for more flexible deployment. Amorphous silicon is very attractive from this viewpoint. In particular, amorphous silicon-coated roof tiles and other photovoltaic materials have been introduced in architectural design and for recreational vehicles, boats, and automobiles.

DEVELOPMENT OF SOLAR CELLS

The development of solar cell technology stems from the work of the French physicist Antoine-César Becquerel in 1839. Becquerel discovered the photovoltaic effect while experimenting with a solid electrode in an electrolyte solution. He observed that voltage developed when light fell upon the electrode. About 50 years later, Charles Fritts constructed the first true solar cells using junctions formed by coating the semiconductor selenium with an ultrathin, nearly transparent layer of gold. Fritts's devices were very inefficient converters of energy, transforming less than 1 percent of absorbed light energy into electrical energy. Though inefficient by today's standards, these early solar cells fostered among some a vision of abundant, clean power. In 1891 R. Appleyard wrote of

> *the blessed vision of the Sun, no longer pouring his energies unrequited into space, but by means of photo-electric cells . . . , these powers gathered into electrical storehouses to the total extinction of steam engines, and the utter repression of smoke.*

By 1927 another metal-semiconductor-junction solar cell, in this case made of copper and the semiconductor copper oxide, had been demonstrated. By the 1930s both the selenium cell and the copper oxide cell were being employed in light-sensitive devices, such as photometers, for use in photography. These early solar cells, however, still had energy-conversion efficiencies of less than 1 percent. This impasse was finally overcome with the development of the silicon solar cell by Russell Ohl in 1941. Thirteen years later, aided by the rapid commercialization of silicon technology needed to fabricate the transistor, three other American researchers—Gerald Pearson, Daryl Chapin, and Calvin Fuller—demonstrated a silicon solar cell capable of a 6 percent energy-conversion efficiency when used in direct sunlight.

By the late 1980s silicon cells, as well as cells made of gallium arsenide, with efficiencies of more than 20 percent, had been fabricated. In 1989 a concentrator solar cell, in which sunlight was concentrated onto the cell surface by means of lenses, achieved an efficiency of 37 percent owing to the increased intensity of the collected energy. By connecting cells of different semiconductors optically and electrically in series, even higher efficiencies are possible, but at increased cost and added complexity. In general, solar cells of widely varying efficiencies and cost are now available.

CHAPTER 2
CHASING THE WIND: WIND ENERGY

Wind is the movement of air over the surface of Earth. Through the use of turbines, the kinetic energy of wind can be converted into mechanical or electrical energy. Wind power is considered a renewable energy source.

Historically, wind has been harnessed by windmills for centuries for such tasks as grinding grain and pumping water. Modern commercial wind turbines produce electrical power by using rotational energy to drive a generator. Wind farms are areas where a number of wind turbines are grouped together, providing a larger total energy source.

WIND POWER

Wind resources are calculated based on the average wind speed and the distribution of wind speed values occurring within a particular area. Areas are grouped into wind power classes that range from 1 to 7. A wind power class of 3 or above (equivalent to a wind power density of 150–200 watts per square metre, or a mean wind of 5.1–5.6 metres [16.7–18.3 feet] per second) is suitable for utility-scale wind power generation, although some suitable sites may also be found in areas of classes 1 and 2. In the United States there are substantial wind resources in the Great Plains region as well as in some offshore locations. As of 2010 the largest wind farm in the world was the Roscoe Wind Farm in Texas, which produces 781.5 megawatts. By comparison,

Windmills on a hillside in California are used to generate electricity. ©
MedioImages/Getty Images

a typical new coal-fired generating plant averages about
550 megawatts.

By the early 21st century, wind was contributing slightly
more than 1 percent of the world's total electricity, and
electricity generation by wind has been increasing dramatically because of concerns over the cost of petroleum
and the effects of fossil fuel combustion on the climate
and environment. From 2004 to 2007, for example, total
wind power increased from 59 to 95 gigawatts worldwide.
During that time period Germany possessed the most
installed wind capacity (16.6 gigawatts), and Denmark
generated the largest percentage of its electricity from
wind (nearly 20 percent). The wind power industry has
estimated that the world could feasibly generate 12

percent of its total electricity from wind power by 2020. Various estimates put the cost of wind energy between 3 and 12 cents per kilowatt-hour, depending on the location. This is comparable to the cost of fossil energy. (The cost of coal-generated electricity is estimated at 4–8 cents per kilowatt-hour.)

Challenges to the large-scale implementation of wind energy include siting requirements such as wind availability, aesthetic and environmental concerns, and land availability. Wind farms are most cost-effective in areas with consistent strong winds. However, these areas are not necessarily near large population centres. Thus, power lines and other components of electrical distribution systems must have the capacity to transmit this electricity to consumers. In addition, since wind is an intermittent and inconsistent power source, storing power may be necessary.

Public advocacy groups have raised concerns about the potential disruptions that wind farms may have on wildlife and overall aesthetics. For example, the first proposed offshore wind farm in the United States, the Cape Wind Project located off the coast of Cape Cod in Massachusetts, was opposed by residents concerned about the natural landscape for nine years before it was finally approved by the federal government in 2010. In addition, wind generators have been blamed for injuring and killing birds. Experts have shown, however, that modern turbines have a small effect on bird populations. The National Audubon Society, a large environmental group based in the United States and focused on the conservation of birds and other wildlife, is strongly in favour of wind power, provided that wind farms are appropriately sited to minimize the impacts on migrating bird populations and important wildlife habitat.

THE HISTORY OF WINDMILLS

Windmills, like waterwheels, were among the original prime movers that replaced animal muscle as a source of power. They were used for centuries in various parts of the world, converting the energy of the wind into mechanical energy for grinding grain, pumping water, and draining lowland areas.

The first known wind device was described by Hero of Alexandria (*c.* 1st century CE). It was modeled on a water-driven paddle wheel and was used to drive a piston pump that forced air through a wind organ to produce sound. The earliest known references to wind-driven grain mills, found in Arabic writings of the 9th century CE, refer to a Persian millwright of 644 CE, although windmills may actually have been used earlier. These mills, erected near what is now the Iran–Afghanistan border, had a vertical shaft with paddlelike sails radiating outward and were located in a building with diametrically opposed openings for the inlet and outlet of the wind. Each mill drove a single set of stones without gearing. The first mills were built with the millstones above the sails, patterned after the early waterwheels from which they were derived. Similar mills were known in China by the 13th century.

Windmills with vertical sails on horizontal shafts reached Europe through contact with the Arabs. Adopting the ideas from contemporary waterwheels, builders began to use fabric-covered, wood-framed sails located above the millstone, instead of a waterwheel below, to drive the grindstone through a set of gears. The whole mill with all its machinery was supported on a fixed post so that it could be rotated and faced into the wind. The millworks were initially covered by a boxlike wooden frame structure and later often by a "round-house," which also provided storage. A brake wheel on the shaft allowed the mill to be stopped by a rim brake. A heavy lever then had to be raised to release the brake, an early example of a fail-safe device. Mills of this sort first appeared in France in 1180, in areas of Syria under the control of the crusaders in 1190, and in England in 1191. The earliest known illustration is from the Windmill Psalter made in Canterbury, Eng., in the second half of the 13th century.

The large effort required to turn a post-mill into the wind probably was responsible for the development of the so-called tower mill in France by the early 14th century. Here, the millstone and the gearing were placed in a massive fixed tower, often circular in section and built of stone or brick. Only an upper cap, normally made of wood and bearing the sails on its shaft, had to be rotated. Such improved mills spread rapidly throughout Europe and later became popular with early American settlers.

The Low Countries of Europe, which had no suitable streams for waterpower, saw the greatest development of windmills. Dutch hollow post-mills, invented in the early 15th century, used a two-step gear drive for drainage pumps. An upright shaft that had gears on the top and bottom passed through the hollow post to drive a paddle-wheel-like scoop to raise water. The first wind-driven sawmill, built in 1592 in the Netherlands by Cornelis Cornelisz, was mounted on a raft to permit easy turning into the wind.

At first both post-mills and the caps of tower mills were turned manually into the wind. Later small posts were placed around the mill to allow winching of the mill with a chain. Eventually winches were placed into the caps of tower mills, engaged with geared racks and operated from inside or from the ground by a chain passing over a wheel. Tower mills had their sail-supporting or tail pole normally inclined at between 5° and 15° to the horizontal. This aided the distribution of the huge sail weight on the tail bearing and also provided greater clearance between the sails and the support structure. Windmills became progressively larger, with sails from about 17 to 24 metres (55.7 to 78.7 feet) in diameter already common in the 16th century. The material of construction, including all gearing, was wood, although eventually brass or gunmetal came into use for the main bearings. Cast-iron drives were first introduced in 1754 by English engineer John Smeaton. Little is known about the actual power produced by these mills. In all likelihood only from 10 to 15 horsepower was developed at the grinding wheels. A 50-horsepower mill was not built until the 19th century. The maximum efficiency of large Dutch mills is estimated to have been about 20 percent.

In 1745 Edmund Lee of England invented the fantail, a ring of five to eight vanes mounted behind the sails at right angles to them. These were connected by gears to wheels running on a track around the cap of the mill. As the wind changed direction, it struck the sides of the fantail vanes, realigning them and thereby turning the main sails again squarely into the wind. Fabric-on-wood-frame sails were sometimes replaced by all-wood sails with removable sections. Early sails had a constant angle of twist; variable twist sails resembling a modern airplane propeller were developed much later.

A major problem with all windmills was the need to feather the sails or reduce sail area so that if the wind suddenly increased during a storm the sails would not be ripped apart. In 1772 Andrew Meikle, a Scottish millwright, invented the spring sail, a shutter arrangement similar to a venetian blind in which the sails were controlled by a spring. When the wind pressure exceeded a preset amount, the shutters opened to let some of the wind pass through. In 1789 Stephen Hooper of England introduced roller blinds that could all be simultaneously adjusted with a manual chain from the ground while the mill was working. This was improved upon in 1807 by Sir William Cubitt, who combined Meikle's shutters with Hooper's remote control by hanging varying weights on the adjustment chain, thus making the control automatic. These so-called patent sails, however, found acceptance only in England and northern Europe.

Even though further improvements were made, especially in speed control, the importance of windmills as a major power producer began to decline after 1784, when the first flour mill in England successfully substituted a steam engine for wind power. Yet, the demise of windmills was slow. These devises persisted throughout the 19th century in newly settled or less-industrialized areas, such as the central and western United States, Canada, Australia, and New Zealand. They also were built by the hundreds in the West Indies to crush sugarcane. At one time in the 19th century there were as many as 900 corn and industrial windmills in the Zaan district of the Netherlands, the highest concentration known.

The primary exception to the steady abandonment of windmills was resurgence in their use in rural areas for pumping water from wells. The first wind pump was introduced in the United States by David Hallay in 1854. After another American, Stewart Perry, began constructing wind pumps made of steel and equipped with metal vanes in 1883, this new and simple device spread around the world.

Wind-driven pumps remain important today in many rural parts of the world. They continued to be used in large numbers, even in the United States, well into the 20th century until low-cost electric power became readily available in rural areas. Although rather inefficient, they are rugged and reliable, need little attention, and remain a prime source for pumping small amounts of water wherever electricity is not economically available.

WIND TURBINES

Modern wind turbines extract energy from the wind, mostly for electricity generation, by rotation of a propeller-like set of blades that drive a generator through appropriate shafts and gears. The older term *windmill* is often still used to describe this type of device, although electric power generation rather than milling has become the primary application.

As was noted earlier, windmills, together with waterwheels, were widely used from the Middle Ages to the 19th century, during the course of which they were supplanted by steam engines and steam turbines. Though they continued to be used for pumping water in rural areas, wind turbines practically disappeared in the 20th century as the internal-combustion engine and electricity provided more reliable and usually less expensive power.

Interest in wind turbines for electricity generation was rekindled by the oil crisis of the mid-1970s. In subsequent decades, concerns over the environment and global warming are what drove renewed awareness of wind turbines as a possible energy source.

HORIZONTAL-AXIS MACHINES

The best-known machines with horizontal axes are the so-called American farm windmills that came into wide use during the 1890s. Such devices consist of a rotor, which may have up to 20 essentially flat sheet-metal blades and a tail vane that keeps the rotor facing into the wind by

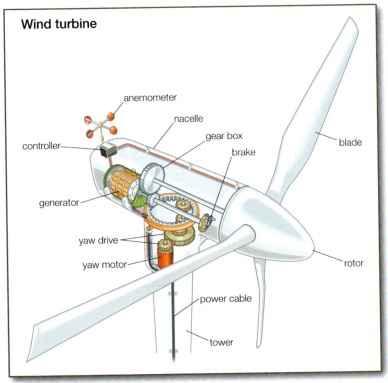

Components of a wind turbine. Encyclopædia Britannica, Inc.

swiveling the entire rotor assembly. Governing is auto-matic and overspeeding is avoided by turning the wheel off the wind direction, thus reducing the effective sail area while keeping the speed constant. A typical pump can deliver about 38 litres (10 gallons) per minute to a height of 30 metres (100 feet) at a wind velocity of 6.7 metres (22 feet) per second.

Modern wind turbines for the generation of elec-tricity have from one to four metal blades that operate at much higher rotor-tip speeds than windmills. They are made up of a blade or rotor and an enclosure called a nacelle that contains a drive train atop a tall tower. Each blade is twisted like an airplane propeller. An automatic governor rotates the blades about their support axis to maintain constant generator speed. The Jacobs three-bladed windmill, used widely between 1930 and 1960, could deliver about one kilowatt of power at a wind speed of 6.25 metres (20.5 feet) per second, a typical average wind velocity in the United States about 18 metres (60 feet) aboveground.

During the 1970s and '80s, a series of large experimental horizontal-shaft, two-bladed turbines were developed in the United States under the sponsorship of the federal government. The first such device, a unit equipped with a rotor measuring 38 metres (125 feet) in diameter, was installed near Sandusky, Ohio, in 1976; its power output was rated at 100 kilowatts. The largest machine was designed (it was never installed) to have a rotor diameter of 122 metres (400 feet) with its axis about 75 metres (250 feet) aboveground. Its output rating was 6.2 megawatts or more at a wind speed of 13 metres (43 feet) per second.

Today, typical large commercial wind turbines, producing up to 2 megawatts of power, can have a blade length of over 40 metres (about 130 feet) and be placed on towers 80 metres (about 260 feet) tall. Smaller turbines can be used to provide power to individual homes.

VERTICAL-AXIS MACHINES

Devices of this kind, which had not been used since the early Middle Ages, found a new application after the Finnish engineer S.J. Savonius invented a new type of rotor in 1922. Known as the Savonius rotor, it consists of semicircular blades that can be constructed from little more than the two sections of an oil drum, cut in half along its vertical axis and welded together with an offset from

A Savonius rotor. Courtesy of Gary Johnson, Ph.D.

the axis to form an open S. An advanced version of this machine installed at Manhattan, Kan., during the 1970s generated five kilowatts of electric power in a 12-metre (40-feet)-per-second wind.

Other vertical wind turbines are based on a machine patented in 1931 by the French engineer G.J.M. Darrieus. Its two blades consist of twisted metal strips tied to the shaft at the top and bottom and bowed out in the middle

A Darrieus wind turbine. Courtesy of the U.S. Department of Energy

similar to the blades on a food mixer. Turbines of this variety are not self-starting and require an external motor for start-up.

A Darrieus turbine with aluminum blades erected in 1980 by the Sandia National Laboratories in New Mexico produced 60 kilowatts in a wind blowing 12.5 metres (41 feet) per second. Several models of Darrieus turbines were built after the construction of the Sandia unit, but vertical-axis turbines have not competed successfully on a commercial scale with horizontal-axis turbines.

CHAPTER 3
HARNESSING WATER: HYDROPOWER

Like air, water is in constant motion over Earth's surface. It can move laterally across the seabed, as in tidal motion, or vertically, as in the motion of ocean swells and waves. This motion, if harnessed properly, can be used to do work.

Humans can also manipulate the motion of water by using devices that trap or redirect the flow. Perhaps the earliest source of mechanical energy to replace that of humans and animals was the waterwheel, a device that taps the energy of running or falling water by means of a set of paddles mounted around a wheel. Waterwheels were gradually replaced beginning in the 19th century by water turbines, which at first were widely used to drive sawmills and textile mill equipment, often through a complex system of gears, shafts, and pulleys. Today, water turbines are used to turn electric generators at hydroelectric dams through the action of falling water.

HYDROELECTRIC POWER

Hydroelectric power is electricity produced from generators driven by water turbines that convert the potential energy in falling or fast-flowing water to mechanical energy.

In the generation of hydroelectric power, water is collected or stored at a higher elevation and led downward through large pipes or tunnels (penstocks) to a lower elevation; the difference in these two elevations is known as the head. At the end of its passage down the pipes, the

An aerial view of the Hoover Dam, on the border of Arizona and Nevada in the United States. Part of the powerhouse is visible at the foot of the U-shaped dam. Shutterstock.com

falling water causes turbines to rotate. The turbines in turn drive generators, which convert the turbines' mechanical energy into electricity. Transformers are then used to convert the alternating voltage suitable for the generators to a higher voltage suitable for long-distance transmission. The structure that houses the turbines and generators, and into which the pipes or penstocks feed, is called the powerhouse.

Hydroelectric power plants are usually located in dams that impound rivers, thereby raising the level of the water behind the dam and creating as high a head as is feasible. The potential power that can be derived from a volume of water is directly proportional to the working head, so that a high-head installation requires a smaller volume of water than a low-head installation to produce an equal amount of power. In some dams, the powerhouse is constructed on one flank of the dam, part of the dam being used as a spillway over which excess water is discharged in times of flood. Where the river flows in a narrow steep gorge, the powerhouse may be located within the dam itself.

In most communities, electric-power demand varies considerably at different times of the day. To even the load on the generators, pumped-storage hydroelectric stations are occasionally built. During off-peak periods, some of the extra power available is supplied to the generator operating as a motor, driving the turbine to pump water into an elevated reservoir. Then, during periods of peak demand, the water is allowed to flow down again through the turbine to generate electrical energy. Pumped-storage systems are efficient and provide an economical way to meet peak loads.

Falling water is one of the three principal traditional sources of energy used to generate electric power, the other two being fossil fuels and nuclear fuels.

THE THREE GORGES DAM

The Three Gorges Dam is located on the Yangtze River (Chang Jiang) just west of the city of Yichang in Hubei province, China. A straight-crested concrete gravity structure, the dam is 2,335 metres (7,660 feet) long with a maximum height of 185 metres (607 feet). It incorporates 28 million cubic metres (37 million cubic yards) of concrete and 463,000 metric tons of steel into its design. When construction of the dam officially began in 1994, it was the largest engineering project in China, and, at the time of its completion in 2006, it was the largest dam structure in the world. Submerging large areas of the Qutang, Wu, and Xilang gorges for some 600 km (375 miles) upstream, the dam is intended to create an immense deepwater reservoir allowing oceangoing freighters to navigate 2,250 km (1,400 miles) inland from Shanghai on the East China Sea to the inland city of Chongqing. Limited hydroelectric power production began in 2003. The dam's 26 existing turbines, in operation since 2008, generate approximately 18 gigawatts of electricity for Shanghai and other cities—as much as that produced by 15 coal-burning power stations. When six more generators are operational in 2011, the dam will generate 22.5 gigawatts of electricity. The dam also is intended to protect millions of people from the periodic flooding that plagues the Yangtze basin.

First discussed in the 1920s by Chinese Nationalist Party leaders, the idea for the Three Gorges Dam was given new impetus in 1953 when Chinese leader Mao Zedong ordered feasibility studies of a number of sites. Detailed planning for the project began in 1955. Its proponents insisted it would control disastrous flooding along the Yangtze, facilitate inland trade, and provide much-needed power for central China, but the dam was not without its detractors. Criticisms of the Three Gorges project began as soon as the plans were proposed and continued through its construction. Key problems included the danger of dam collapse, the displacement of some 1.2 million people (critics insisted the figure was actually 1.9 million) living in nearly 500 cities, towns, and villages along the river, and the destruction of

magnificent scenery and countless rare architectural and archaeological sites. There were also fears that human and industrial
waste from Chongqing and other cities would pollute the reservoir and even that the huge amount of water impounded in
the reservoir could trigger earthquakes and landslides. Some
Chinese and foreign engineers argued that a number of smaller
and far-cheaper and less-problematic dams on the Yangtze
tributaries could generate as much power as the Three Gorges
Dam and control flooding equally as well. Construction of those
dams, they maintained, would enable the government to meet
its main priorities without the risks.

Because of these problems, work on the Three Gorges Dam
was delayed for nearly 40 years as the Chinese government
struggled to reach a decision to carry through with plans for the
project. In 1992 Premier Li Peng, who had himself trained as
an engineer, was finally able to persuade the National People's
Congress to ratify the decision to build the dam, though almost
a third of its members abstained or voted against the project—
an unprecedented sign of resistance from a normally acquiescent
body. Pres. Jiang Zemin did not accompany Li to the official
inauguration of the dam in 1994, and the World Bank refused
to advance China funds to help with the project, citing major
environmental and other concerns.

Nevertheless, the Three Gorges project moved ahead. In
1993 work started on access roads and electricity to the site.
Workers blocked and diverted the river in 1997, bringing to a
close the first phase of construction. In 2003 the reservoir began
to fill, the navigation locks were put into preliminary operation,
and the first of the dam's generators was connected to the grid,
completing the second phase of construction. (Following completion of this second phase, some 1,200 sites of historical and
archaeological importance that once lined the middle reaches of
the Yangtze River vanished as floodwaters rose.) Construction
of the main wall of the dam was completed in 2006.

Hydroelectric power has certain advantages over these other sources: it is continually renewable owing to the recurring nature of the hydrologic cycle and produces neither atmospheric nor thermal pollution. Hydroelectric power is a preferred energy source in areas with heavy rainfall and with hilly or mountainous regions that are in reasonably close proximity to the main load centres. Some large hydro sites that are remote from load centres may be sufficiently attractive to justify the long high-voltage transmission lines. Small local hydro sites may also be economical, particularly if they combine storage of water during light loads with electricity production during peaks.

TIDAL POWER AND WAVE POWER

In addition to falling through the sluices of a dam, water has been captured by new devices that are making tidal power and wave power major new players in the electric power scene. Tidal power is a form of renewable energy in which tidal action in the oceans is converted to electric power. Wave power is the generation of electricity through the harnessing of the up-and-down motion of ocean waves.

There are a number of ways in which tidal power can be harnessed. Tidal barrage power systems take advantage of differences between high tides and low tides by using a "barrage," or type of dam, to trap water that has flowed into the system during high-tide periods. As the tide ebbs, the trapped water is released and passes through a turbine that generates electricity; a similar process occurs in hydroelectric dams. Tidal stream power systems take advantage of ocean currents to drive turbines, particularly in areas around islands or coasts where these currents are fast. They can be installed as tidal fences, where turbines are stretched across a channel, or as tidal turbines, which resemble underwater wind turbines.

Wave power is typically produced by floating turbine platforms. However, it can be generated by exploiting the changes in air pressure occurring in wave-capture chambers that face the sea. Wave power systems can be installed in shoreline areas as well as offshore. Generally, the areas of greatest potential for wave energy development are the latitudes with the highest winds (latitudes 40°–60° N and S) on the eastern shores of the world's oceans. For this reason a large potential for wave power systems exists in the British Isles and the Pacific Northwest of the United States.

Many tidal power technologies are not available at an industrial scale, and thus tidal energy contributes a negligible fraction of global energy today. There is, however, a large potential for its use, because much usable energy is contained in water currents. The total energy contained in tides worldwide is 3,000 gigawatts (GW; billion watts), though estimates of how much of that energy is available for power generation by tidal barrages are between 120 and 400 GW, depending on the location and the potential for conversion. By comparison, a typical new coal-based generating plant produces about 550 megawatts (MW; million watts). For wave energy, one estimate is 2,000 terawatt-hours per year (approximately 10 percent of global electricity production), and tidal stream power—which uses ocean currents to drive underwater blades in a manner similar to wind power generation—in shallow water can generate some 3,800 terawatt-hours per year (one terawatt is 1×10^{12} watts).

By the early 21st century, some of these technologies had become commercially available. A tidal barrage

A boat circles near a wave-power generator off the Atlantic coast of Portugal. The floating tubes bob in the waves, powering attached generators. Joao Abreu Miranda/AFP/Getty Images

power station at La Rance in France began operating in the 1960s, with 240 MW of capacity. Its typical output is 0.5 terawatt-hour per year. Because few tidal current plants exist, the costs of this technology are not known, but it is expected that costs would be lower than for tidal barrage systems. The world's first operational wave-power generator is located off the coast of Aguçadora, Port., producing as much as 2.25 megawatts from three huge jointed tubes that float on the surface of the Atlantic Ocean; individual power generators are located at the tubes' joints and are activated by wave motion.

Environmental concerns raised about tidal power stations are largely focused on the tidal barrage systems, which can disrupt estuarine ecosystems during their construction and operation. Tidal fences and turbines are expected to have minimal impact on ocean ecosystems. Tidal fences do have the potential to injure or kill migratory fish, however, but these structures can be designed to minimize such effects.

WATERWHEELS

Waterwheels were the earliest machines. First used for grinding grain, they were subsequently adopted to drive sawmills and pumps, to provide the bellows action for furnaces and forges, to drive tilt hammers or trip-hammers for forging iron, and to provide direct mechanical power for textile mills. Until the development of steam power during the Industrial Revolution at the end of the 18th century, waterwheels were the primary means of mechanical power production, rivaled only occasionally by windmills. Thus, many industrial towns, especially in early America, sprang up at locations where water flow could be assured all year.

The oldest reference to a water mill dates to about 85 BCE, appearing in a poem by an early Greek writer celebrating the liberation from toil of the young women who operated the querns (primitive hand mills) for grinding corn. According to the Greek geographer Strabo, King Mithradates VI of Pontus in Asia used a hydraulic machine, presumably a water mill, by about 65 BCE.

Early vertical-shaft water mills drove querns where the wheel, containing radial vanes or paddles and rotating in a horizontal plane, could be lowered into the stream. The vertical shaft was connected through a hole in the stationary grindstone to the upper, or rotating, stone. The device spread rapidly from Greece to other parts of the world, because it was easy to build and maintain and could operate in any fast-flowing stream. It was known in China by the 1st century CE, was used throughout Europe by the end of the 3rd century, and had reached Japan by the year 610. Users learned early that performance could be improved with a millrace and a chute that would direct the water to one side of the wheel.

A horizontal-shaft water mill was first described by the Roman architect and engineer Vitruvius about 27 BCE. It consisted of an undershot waterwheel in which water enters below the centre of the wheel and is guided by a millrace and chute. The waterwheel was coupled with a right-angle gear drive to a vertical-shaft grinding wheel. This type of mill became popular throughout the Roman Empire, notably in Gaul, after the advent of Christianity led to the freeing of slaves and the resultant need for an alternative source of power. Early large waterwheels, which measured about 1.8 metres (six feet) in diameter, are estimated to have produced about three horsepower, the largest amount of power produced by any machine of the time. The Roman mills were adopted throughout much of medieval Europe, and waterwheels of increasing size, made almost entirely of wood, were built until the 18th century.

In addition to flowing stream water, ocean tides were used to drive waterwheels. Tidal water was allowed to flow into large millponds, controlled initially through lock-type gates and later through flap valves. Once the tide ebbed, water was let out through sluice gates and directed onto the wheel. Sometimes the tidal flow was assisted by building a dam across the estuary of a small river. Although limited in operation to ebbing tide conditions, tidal mills were widely used by the 12th century. The earliest recorded reference to tidal mills is found in the *Domesday Book* (1086), which also records more than 5,000 water mills in England south of the Severn and Trent rivers. (Tidal mills also were built along the Atlantic coast in Europe and centuries later on the eastern seaboard of the United States and in Guyana, where they powered sugarcane-crushing mills.)

The first analysis of the performance of waterwheels was published in 1759 by John Smeaton, an English engineer. Smeaton built a test apparatus with a small wheel (its diameter was only 0.61 metre) to measure the effects of water velocity, as well as head and wheel speed. He found that the maximum efficiency (work produced divided by potential energy in the water) he could obtain was 22 percent for an undershot wheel and 63 percent for an overshot wheel (i.e., one in which water enters the wheel above its centre). In 1776 Smeaton became the first to use a cast-iron wheel, and two years later he introduced cast-iron gearing, thereby bringing to an end the all-wood construction that had prevailed since Roman times. Based on his model tests, Smeaton built an undershot wheel for the London Bridge waterworks that measured 4.6 metres (15 feet) wide and that had a diameter of 9.75 metres (32 feet). The results of Smeaton's experimental work came to be widely used throughout Europe for designing new wheels.

During the mid-1700s a reaction waterwheel for generating small amounts of power became popular in the rural areas of England. In this type of device, commonly known as a Barker's mill, water flowed into a rotating vertical tube before being discharged through nozzles at the end of two horizontal arms. These directed the water out tangentially, much in the way that a modern rotary lawn sprinkler does. A rope or belt wound around the vertical tube provided the power takeoff.

Early in the 19th century Jean-Victor Poncelet, a French mathematician and engineer, designed curved paddles for undershot wheels to allow the water to enter smoothly. His design was based on the idea that water would run up the surface of the curved vanes, come to rest at the inner diameter, and then fall away with practically no velocity.

This design increased the efficiency of undershot wheels to 65 percent. At about the same time, William Fairbairn, a Scottish engineer, showed that breast wheels (i.e., those in which water enters at the 10- or two-o'clock position) were more efficient than overshot wheels and less vulnerable to flood damage. He used curved buckets and provided a close-fitting masonry wall to keep the water from flowing out sideways. In 1828 Fairbairn introduced ventilated buckets in which gaps at the bottom of each bucket allowed trapped air to escape. Other improvements included a governor to control the sluice gates and spur gearing for the power takeoff.

During the course of the 19th century, waterwheels were slowly supplanted by water turbines. Water turbines were more efficient; design improvements eventually made it possible to regulate the speed of the turbines and to run them fast enough to drive electric generators. This fact notwithstanding, waterwheels gave way slowly, and it was not until the early 20th century that they became largely obsolescent. Yet, even today some waterwheels still survive. Equipped with submerged bearings, these modern waterwheels certainly are more sophisticated than their predecessors, though they bear a remarkable likeness to them.

WATER TURBINES

Water turbines are the modern successors of simple waterwheels. A water turbine uses the potential energy resulting from the difference in elevation between an upstream water reservoir and the turbine-exit water level (the tailrace) to convert this so-called head into work. Today, most water turbines are used for generating electricity in hydroelectric installations.

Water turbines are generally divided into two categories: (1) impulse turbines used for high heads of water and low flow rates and (2) reaction turbines normally employed for heads below about 450 metres and moderate or high flow rates. These two classes include the main types in common use—namely, the Pelton impulse turbine and the reaction turbines of the Francis, propeller, Kaplan, and Deriaz variety. Turbines can be arranged with either horizontal or, more commonly, vertical shafts. Wide design variations are possible within each type to meet the specific local hydraulic conditions.

IMPULSE TURBINES

In an impulse turbine the potential energy, or the head of water, is first converted into kinetic energy by discharging

A vintage Pelton waterwheel—used by Pacific Gas and Light for decades— stands as a monument at the site of the apparatus's first commercial manufacturing facility in Nevada City, California. Russ Bishop Photography/Newscom

water through a carefully shaped nozzle. The jet, discharged into air, is directed onto curved buckets fixed on the periphery of the runner to extract the water energy and convert it to useful work.

Modern impulse turbines are based on a design patented in 1889 by the American engineer Lester Allen Pelton. The free water jet strikes the turbine buckets tangentially. Each bucket has a high centre ridge so that the flow is divided to leave the runner at both sides. Pelton wheels are suitable for high heads, typically above about 450 metres (1,476 feet) with relatively low water flow rates. For maximum efficiency the runner tip speed should equal about one-half the striking jet velocity. The efficiency (work produced by the turbine divided by the kinetic energy of the free jet) can exceed 91 percent when operating at 60–80 percent of full load.

The power of a given wheel can be increased by using more than one jet. Two-jet arrangements are common for horizontal shafts. Sometimes two separate runners are mounted on one shaft driving a single electric generator. Vertical-shaft units may have four or more separate jets.

If the electric load on the turbine changes, its power output must be rapidly adjusted to match the demand. This requires a change in the water flow rate to keep the generator speed constant. The flow rate through each nozzle is controlled by a centrally located, carefully shaped spear or needle that slides forward or backward as controlled by a hydraulic servomotor.

Proper needle design assures that the velocity of the water leaving the nozzle remains essentially the same irrespective of the opening, assuring nearly constant efficiencies over much of the operating range. It is not prudent to reduce the water flow suddenly to match a load decrease. This could lead to a destructive pressure surge (water hammer) in the supply pipeline, or penstock. Such surges can be avoided by adding a temporary spill nozzle that opens while the main nozzle closes or, more commonly, by partially inserting a deflector plate between the jet and the wheel, diverting and dissipating some of the energy while the needle is slowly closed.

Another type of impulse turbine is the turgo type. The jet impinges at an oblique angle on the runner from one side and continues in a single path, discharging at the other side of the runner. This type of turbine has been used in medium-sized units for moderately high heads.

REACTION TURBINES

In a reaction turbine, forces driving the rotor are achieved by the reaction of an accelerating water flow in the runner while the pressure drops. The reaction principle can be observed in a rotary lawn sprinkler where the emerging jet drives the rotor in the opposite direction. Due to the great variety of possible runner designs, reaction turbines can be used over a much larger range of heads and flow rates than impulse turbines. Reaction turbines typically have a spiral inlet casing that includes control gates to regulate the water flow. In the inlet a fraction of the potential energy of the water may be converted to kinetic energy as the flow accelerates. The water energy is subsequently extracted in the rotor.

There are, as noted above, four major kinds of reaction turbines in wide use: the Kaplan, Francis, Deriaz, and propeller type. In fixed-blade propeller and adjustable-blade Kaplan turbines (named after the Austrian inventor Victor Kaplan), there is essentially an axial flow through the machine. The Francis- and Deriaz-type turbines (after the British-born American inventor James B.

Francis and the Swiss engineer Paul Deriaz, respectively) use a "mixed flow," where the water enters radially inward and discharges axially. Runner blades on Francis and propeller turbines consist of fixed blading, while in Kaplan and Deriaz turbines the blades can be rotated about their axis, which is at right angles to the main shaft.

AXIAL-FLOW MACHINES

Fixed propeller-type turbines are generally used for large units at low heads, resulting in large diameters and slow rotational speeds. As the name suggests, a propeller-type turbine runner looks like the very large propeller of a ship except that it serves the opposite purpose: power is extracted in a turbine, whereas it is fed into a marine propeller. The central shaft, or hub, may have the propeller blades bolted to it during on-site assembly, thus permitting shipment by sections for a large runner. At low heads (below about 24 metres [78 feet]), vertical-shaft propeller turbines typically have a concrete spiral inlet casing of rectangular cross section. Inlet guide vanes are either mounted on a ring or, in large units, set individually directly into the concrete. The flow passage can be increased or decreased by servomotor-driven wicket gates. The kinetic energy leaving the runner can be partially recaptured by a draft tube, a conical diffusing exit section where the velocity is decreased while the pressure is increased. This leads to improved efficiency by keeping the loss of kinetic energy in the exit, or tail, section of the installation to a minimum.

Propeller turbines are used extensively in North America, where low heads and large flow rates are common. For example, there are 32 propeller turbines in the Moses–Saunders Power Dam on the St. Lawrence River between New York and Ontario—16 operated by the

Canadian and U.S. entities split operation of the 32 propellor turbines that power the Robert Moses–Robert H. Saunders Power Dam on the St. Lawrence River. © AP Images

United States and 16 by Canada, with each turbine rated at 50 megawatts. With such large plants it is possible to run each turbine at or near its most efficient output by switching complete units in or out as the load fluctuates, in addition to regulating each unit.

If the head or the water flow rate tends to vary seasonally, as occurs in many river systems, an installation with only a few propeller turbines might have to operate all units at partial output under average flow and load conditions. The energy-conversion efficiency of a conventional propeller turbine decreases rapidly once the turbine load drops below 75 percent of its rating. This performance loss can be minimized by varying the inlet-blade angle of the runner to match the runner-inlet conditions more accurately with the water velocity for a given flow. In such a Kaplan turbine each blade can be swiveled about a post at right angles to the main turbine shaft, thus producing a variable pitch. The angle of the blades is controlled by an oil-pressure operated servomotor, usually mounted in the rotor hub with the oil fed through the generator and turbine shaft. The servo-control system, which also drives the gates through a cam or rocker arrangement, is designed to adjust angles and inlet flows to match the electrical load while keeping the main shaft with its directly coupled generator rotating at constant speed. Runners with four to six blades are common, though more blades may be used for high heads. British manufacturers have developed Kaplan designs for heads up to 58 metres (190 feet).

Although the usual turbine installation has a vertical shaft, some also have been designed with horizontal shafts. In a horizontal bulb arrangement, the generator is embedded in a nacelle, corresponding to the thick body of a light bulb, while the blades are set around a hub corresponding to the thinner bulb socket. This design is suitable for medium-sized machines operating at very low heads when an almost straight-through water flow is desirable. The Rance River tidal plant in France employs this kind of arrangement.

MIXED-FLOW TURBINES

Francis turbines are probably used most extensively because of their wider range of suitable heads, characteristically from 3 to 600 metres (10 to 2,000 feet). At the high-head range, the flow rate and the output must be large; otherwise the runner becomes too small for reasonable fabrication. At the low-head end, propeller turbines are usually more efficient unless the power output is also small. Francis turbines reign supreme in the medium-head range of 120 to 300 metres (400 to 1,000 feet) and come in a wide range of designs and sizes. They can have either horizontal or vertical shafts, the latter being used for machines with diameters of about two metres (six feet) or more. Vertical-shaft machines usually occupy less space than horizontal units, permit greater submergence of the runner with a minimum of deep excavation, and make the tip-mounted generator more easily accessible for maintenance. Horizontal-shaft units are more compact for smaller sizes and allow easier access to the turbine, although removal of the generator for repair becomes more difficult as size increases.

The most common form of Francis turbine has a welded, or cast-steel, spiral casing. The casing distributes water evenly to all inlet gates; up to 24 pivoted gates or guide vanes have been used. The gates operate from fully closed to wide open, depending on the power output desired. Most are driven by a common regulating speed ring and are pin-connected in such a fashion that no damage will occur if debris blocks one of the gate passages. The regulating ring is rotated by one or two oil-pressure servomotors that are controlled by the speed governor.

Slow, high-power units have a nearly radial set of blades, while in fast and lower-powered units the curved blades reach from the radial inlet to almost the axial outlet. Once the overall blade dimensions (inlet and exit diameters and blade height) have been defined, the blades are designed for a smooth entry of the water flow at the inlet and minimum water swirl at the exit. The number of blades can vary from seven to 19. Runners for low-head units are usually made of cast mild steel, sometimes with stainless-steel protection added at locations subject to cavitation. All stainless-steel construction is more commonly used for high heads. Large units can be welded together on-site, using an appropriate combination of various preformed steel sections to provide carefully shaped, finished water passages. Francis turbines allow for very large, high-output units. The Grand Coulee hydroelectric power plant on the Columbia River in Washington State has the largest single runner in the United States, a device capable of producing 716 megawatts at a head of 93 metres. The Itaipú plant on the Paraná River between Brazil and Paraguay has 18 Francis turbines capable of producing 740 megawatts each at heads between 118.4 and 126.7 metres (388.5 and 415.7 feet) while rotating at slightly above 90 revolutions per minute.

A mixed-flow turbine of the Deriaz type uses swiveled, variable-pitch runner blades that allow for improved efficiency at part loads in medium-sized machines. The Deriaz design has proved useful for higher heads and also for some pumped storage applications. It has the advantage of a lower runaway (sudden loss of load) speed than a Kaplan turbine, which results in significant savings in generator costs. Very few Deriaz turbines, however, have actually been built. The first non-reversible Deriaz turbine, capable of producing 22.75 megawatts with a head of 55 metres (180 feet), was installed in an underground station at Culligran, Scot., in 1958.

OUTPUT AND SPEED CONTROL

If the load on the generator is decreased, a turbine will tend to speed up unless the flow rate can be reduced accordingly. Similarly, an increase of load will cause the turbine to slow down unless more water can be admitted. Since electric-generator speeds must be kept constant to a high degree of precision, this leads to complex controls. These must take into account the large masses and inertias of the metal and the flowing water, including the water in the inflow pipes (or penstocks), that will be affected by any change in the wicket gate setting. If the inlet pipeline is long, the closing time of the wicket gate must be slow enough to keep the pressure increase caused by a reduction in flow velocity within acceptable limits. If the closing or opening rate is too slow, control instabilities may result. To assist regulation with long pipelines, a surge chamber is often connected to the pipeline as close to the turbine as possible. This enables part of the water in the line to pass into the surge chamber when the wicket gates are rapidly closed or opened. Medium-sized reaction turbines may also be provided with pressure-relief valves through which some water can be bypassed automatically as the governor starts to close the turbine. In some applications, both relief valves and surge chambers have been used.

CAVITATION

According to Bernoulli's principle (derived by the Swiss mathematician Daniel Bernoulli), as the flow velocity of the water increases at any given elevation, the pressure will drop. There is a danger that in high-velocity sections of a reaction turbine, especially near the exit, the pressure can become so low that the water flashes over into small vapour bubbles, which then collapse suddenly. This so-called cavitation leads to erosion pitting as well as to vibrations and must be avoided by the careful shaping of all blade passages and of the exit passage or draft tube.

TURBINE SELECTION ON THE BASIS OF SPECIFIC SPEED

Initial turbine selection is usually based on the ratio of design variables known as the power specific speed. In U.S. design practice this is given by the formula

$$N = \frac{n P^{1/2}}{H^{5/4}},$$

where n is in revolutions per minute, P is the output in horsepower, and H is the head of water in feet. Turbine types can be classified by their specific speed, N, which always applies at the point of maximum efficiency. If N ranges from one to 20, corresponding to high heads and low rotational speeds, impulse turbines are appropriate. For N between 10 and 90, Francis-type runners should be selected, with slow-running, near-radial units for the lower N values and more rapidly rotating mixed-flow runners for higher N values. For N up to 110, Deriaz turbines may be suitable. If N ranges from 70 to the maximum of 260, propeller or Kaplan turbines are called for.

Using the specific speed formula, a turbine designed to deliver 100,000 horsepower (74.6 megawatts) with a head of 40 feet (12.2 metres) operating at 72 revolutions per minute would have a specific speed of 226, suggesting a propeller or Kaplan turbine. It can also be shown that the flow rate would have to be about 24,500 cubic feet per second (694 cubic metres per second) at a turbine efficiency of 90 percent. The runner diameter will be about 33 feet (10 metres). This illustrates the large sizes required for high-power, low-head installations and the low rotational speed at which these turbines have to operate to stay within the permissible specific speed range.

TURBINE MODEL TESTING

Before building large-scale installations, the design should be checked out with turbine model tests, using geometrically similar models of small and intermediate size, all operating at the same specific speed. Allowances must be made for the effects of friction, determined by the Reynolds number (density × rotational speed × runner diameter squared/viscosity) and for possible changes in scaled roughness and clearance dimensions. Friction effects are less important for large units, which tend to be more efficient than smaller ones.

CHAPTER 4
TAPPING THE EARTH: GEOTHERMAL ENERGY

Geothermal energy is power obtained by using heat from the Earth's interior. Most geothermal resources are in regions of active volcanism. Hot springs, geysers, pools of boiling mud, and fumaroles (vents of volcanic gases and heated groundwater) are the most easily exploited sources of such energy. The ancient Romans used hot springs to heat baths and homes, and similar uses are still found in some geothermal regions of the world, such as Iceland, Turkey, and Japan.

The greatest potential for geothermal energy, however, lies in the generation of electricity. Geothermal energy was first used to produce electric power at Larderello, Italy, in 1904. By the late 20th century, geothermal power plants were in operation in Italy, New Zealand, Japan, Iceland, Mexico, the United States, and elsewhere, and many others were under construction in other countries.

The most useful geothermal resources are hot water and steam trapped in subsurface formations or reservoirs and having temperatures ranging from 80 to 350 °C (176 to 662 °F). Water and steam hotter than 180 °C (356 °F) are the most easily exploited for electric-power generation and are utilized by most existing geothermal power plants. In these plants the hot water is flashed to steam, which is then used to drive a turbine whose mechanical energy is then converted to electricity by a generator. In some systems part of the steam is condensed back to liquid water and then injected into the subsurface reservoir for reheating and reconversion to steam.

The development of geothermal resources is attractive owing to the cost of petroleum and the nonpolluting character of geothermal energy production. However, usable sites are relatively scarce, and over time there is a risk of depleting the subsurface steam reservoirs.

HOT SPRINGS

Hot springs, also called thermal springs, are springs with water at temperatures substantially higher than the air temperature of the surrounding region. Most hot springs discharge groundwater that is heated by shallow intrusions of magma (molten rock) in volcanic areas. Some thermal springs, however, are not related to volcanic activity. In such cases, the water is heated by convective circulation. Groundwater percolating downward reaches depths of a kilometre or more, where the temperature of rocks is high because of the normal temperature gradient of the Earth's crust—about 30 °C per kilometre in the first 10 km (roughly 90 °F per mile in the first 6 miles).

Many of the colours in hot springs are caused by thermophilic (heat-loving) microorganisms. The cyanobacteria, one of the more common of these groups, grow in huge colonies called bacterial mats that form the colourful scums and slimes on the sides of hot springs. Various colours of cyanobacteria prefer specific conditions of water chemistry and temperature, thus providing a rough "thermometer" for hot springs: yellow, about 70 °C (160 °F); brown, about 60 °C (140 °F); and green, about 50 °C (120 °F) or lower.

A tremendous amount of heat is released by hot springs, and various applications of this geothermal energy have been developed. In certain areas, buildings and greenhouses are heated with water pumped from hot springs.

Yellowstone National Park in the United States is one of the most famous areas of hot springs and geysers in the world. The total heat flux from these thermal features is estimated to be 300 megawatts (300 million watts). The last great eruption at Yellowstone occurred about 630,000 years ago when some 1,000 cubic km (240 cubic miles) of rhyolitic pumice and ash were ejected in huge pyroclastic flows and resulted in the formation of a caldera—a large circular or oval depression caused by collapse of the surface following magma removal—approximately 45 by 75 km (28 by 47 miles) in size. Yellowstone Lake now occupies part of this giant caldera. Since that last great outburst, about 1,200 cubic km (288 cubic miles) of rhyolite lava flows and domes have erupted in numerous smaller events. The cooling roots of such past eruptions, or possibly the new intrusions of magma at shallow depth, are the heat sources for the Yellowstone hot springs and geysers.

HOT SPRINGS, ARKANSAS

Hot Springs is a resort and spa located in central Arkansas, U.S. It lies just north of the Ouachita River at the eastern edge of the Ouachita Mountains and the Ouachita National Forest. Hot Springs National Park is intertwined with the northern portion of the city.

The area is noted for its numerous thermal springs, which were long used by Native Americans and probably were visited by the Spanish explorer Hernando de Soto in 1541. French fur trappers and traders frequented the springs from the late 17th century, and the area was mapped in 1804 by an expedition led by the Americans William Dunbar and George Hunter. Permanent settlement of the site dates from 1807.

Hot Springs National Park originated in 1832 as Hot Springs Reservation on land set aside by the federal government. Later enlarged, it became a national park in 1921 and today covers 23 square km (9 square miles). Central to the park are the 47 hot springs and 8 historic bathhouses along Central Avenue (also called Bathhouse Row) located on the southwestern slope of Hot Springs Mountain. Water from the hot springs flows at a rate of 3,200,000 litres (850,000 gallons) per day, with an average temperature of 62 °C (143 °F). Originally each of the bathhouses along Bathhouse Row had its own spring, but today the water is collected for common distribution to the restored Buckstaff Bathhouse (the one remaining active bathhouse along the row), four hotel bathhouses, and several medical facilities. The Fordyce Bathhouse, also located along Bathhouse Row, has been restored to look as it did between 1915 and 1920; it is the park's visitor centre. The exteriors of the other six historic bathhouses also have been restored. The surrounding Zig Zag Mountains that make up the park area beyond Bathhouse Row are heavily forested in oak, hickory, and pine, with stands of dogwood, redbud, and other flowering species. Wildlife is abundant and consists primarily of small mammals and numerous species of birds.

The town of Hot Springs was incorporated in 1876 and became a city in 1886. Its population grew with the rise in popularity of the springs. Among the numerous hotels and bathhouses that sprang up in the area were those built outside the federal park, and in the 1920s and '30s many of these were frequented by such gangsters as Al Capone and George ("Bugs") Moran. As the number of visitors declined after 1950, most of the establishments closed. Tourism, however, has remained important.

GEYSERS

Geysers are hot springs that intermittently spout a column of hot water and steam into the air. The term is derived from the Icelandic word *geysir*, meaning "to gush."

The spouting action is caused by the water in deep conduits beneath a geyser approaching or reaching the boiling point. Groundwater percolates through porous rock into fractures deep underground, where heat from a nearby magma chamber superheats the pressurized water to a temperature above the boiling point of water at surface pressure. At 300 metres (about 1,000 feet) below the surface, the boiling point of water increases to approximately 230 °C (450 °F) because of the increased pressure of the overlying water.

In hot springs the rising superheated water is cooled below the boiling point by groundwater before reaching the surface. In geysers the superheated water collects in underground pockets. As bubbles of steam or dissolved gas begin to form, rise, and expand, hot water spills from the geyser's vent, lowering the pressure on the water column below. Water at depth then momentarily exceeds its boiling point and flashes into steam, forcing additional water from the vent and ejecting a column of steam and water into the air. This chain reaction continues until the geyser exhausts its supply of boiling water.

After a geyser stops spouting, the conduits at depth refill with groundwater, and reheating begins again. In geysers such as Yellowstone's Old Faithful, the spouting and recharge period is quite regular. This famous geyser has gushed to heights of 30 to 55 metres (100 to 180 feet) about every 90 minutes for more than 100 years. If Old Faithful's eruption lasts only a minute or two, the next interval will be shorter than average, while a four-minute

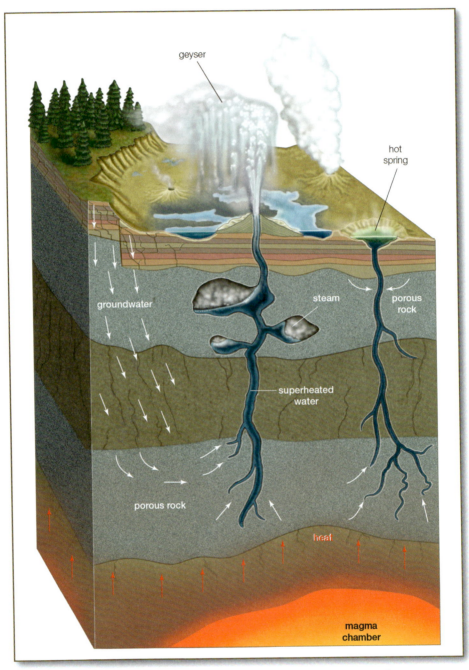

Cross section of a geyser and hot spring. Encyclopædia Britannica, Inc.

eruption will be followed by a longer interval. Other geysers have much more erratic recharge times.

Geysers are generally associated with areas that have seen past volcanic activity. Geothermal power from steam wells depends on the same volcanic heat sources and boiling temperature changes with depth that drive geyser displays.

As water is ejected from geysers and cooled, dissolved silica is precipitated in mounds on the surface. This material is known as sinter. Often geysers have been given fanciful names (such as Castle Geyser) inspired by the shapes of the colourful and contorted mounds of siliceous sinter at the vents.

Geysers are rare. There are about 500 of them in Yellowstone National Park in the western United States, about 200 on the Kamchatka Peninsula in Russia, about

Old Faithful geyser, Upper Geyser Basin, Yellowstone National Park, Wyoming, U.S. George Marler/National Park Service

40 in New Zealand, 16 in Iceland, and another 50 scattered throughout the world in many other volcanic areas.

GEOTHERMAL POWER

Geothermal energy is plentiful, but geothermal power is not. Temperatures increase below the Earth's surface at a rate of about 30 °C per km in the first 10 km (roughly 90 °F per mile in the first 6 miles) below the surface. This internal heat of the Earth is an immense store of energy. In the upper 10 km of rock beneath the conterminous United States, it amounts to 3.3×10^{25} joules, or about 6,000 times the energy contained in the world's oil reserves. The problem in utilizing geothermal energy is extracting it.

The natural escape of the Earth's heat through its surface averages only 0.06 watt per square metre (0.006 watt per square foot). To make geothermal power practical, some special situation must exist to concentrate the Earth's heat energy in a small area. Underground reservoirs of steam or hot water that can be funneled into a drill hole provide this special situation. Some geothermal steam wells can produce 25 megawatts of thermal power, an amount equal to the normal heat flux of more than 400 square km (150 square miles) of land surface. The key to this concentration is the transfer of heat from deeper levels to the near surface by the ascending magma associated with volcanism. Magma at temperatures close to 1,200 °C (2,200 °F) moves upward to depths of only a few kilometres, where it transfers heat by conduction to groundwater. The groundwater then circulates by convection and forms large underground reservoirs of hot water and steam. Some of this thermal water may escape to the surface as hot springs or geysers.

Holes drilled into a subsurface geothermal system allow rapid transfer of hot water or steam to the surface.

At the Geysers, a geothermal field north of San Francisco, superheated steam is directly tapped from porous underground reservoirs. After the steam has been passed through turbines, some of it is condensed back into liquid water and pumped back underground to be reheated into steam. In addition, treated wastewater piped in from some municipalities in California is injected into the reservoirs. In most other geothermal fields, the hot water is at or below its subsurface boiling temperature—about 300 °C (570 °F) at a depth of 1 km (0.6 mile). The hot water and steam produced from geothermal wells are used as the energy source to drive turbine generators in electric power plants. Hot water from lower-temperature geothermal reservoirs can be used for space heating and other applications. This form of geothermal power is utilized extensively in Iceland.

Some geothermal systems act as natural distilleries in the subsurface, dissolving trace amounts of gold, silver, and other rare elements from their host rocks. These elements may then be deposited at places where changes in temperature, pressure, or composition favour precipitation. Many hydrothermal ore deposits have been formed by once active—and in a few cases still active—geothermal systems.

STEAM TURBINES

A steam turbine consists of a rotor resting on bearings and enclosed in a cylindrical casing. The rotor is turned by steam impinging against attached vanes or blades on which it exerts a force in the tangential direction. Thus a steam turbine could be viewed as a complex series of windmill-like arrangements, all assembled on the same shaft.

Because of its ability to develop tremendous power within a comparatively small space, the steam turbine has superseded all other prime movers, except hydraulic tur-bines, for generating large amounts of electricity and for providing propulsive power for large, high-speed ships. Today, units capable of generating more than 1.3 million kilowatts of power can be mounted on a single shaft.

PRINCIPAL COMPONENTS

The main parts of a steam turbine are (1) the rotor that car-ries the blading to convert the thermal energy of the steam into the rotary motion of the shaft, (2) the casing, inside of which the rotor turns, that serves as a pressure vessel for containing the steam (it also accommodates fixed nozzle passages or stator vanes through which the steam is accel-erated before being directed against and through the rotor blading), (3) the speed-regulating mechanism, and (4) the support system, which includes the lubrication system for the bearings that support the rotor and also absorb any end thrust developed.

BLADING DESIGN

The turbine blading must be carefully designed with the correct aerodynamic shape to properly turn the flow-ing steam and generate rotational energy efficiently. The blades also have to be strong enough to withstand high centrifugal stresses and must be sized to avoid dangerous vibrations. Various types of blading arrangements have been proposed, but all are designed to take advantage of the principle that when a given mass of steam suddenly changes its velocity, a force is then exerted by the mass in direct proportion to the rate of change of velocity.

Two types of blading have been developed to a high degree of perfection: impulse blading and reaction blad-ing. In impulse blading a series of stationary nozzles allows

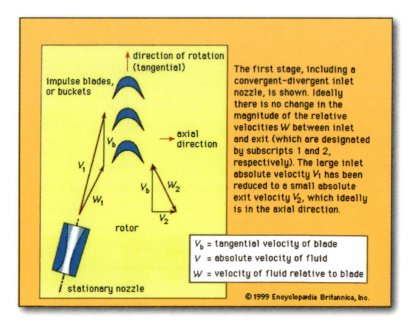

The first stage, including a convergent-divergent inlet nozzle, is shown. Ideally there is no change in the magnitude of the relative velocities W between inlet and exit (which are designated by subscripts 1 and 2, respectively). The large inlet absolute velocity V_1 has been reduced to a small absolute exit velocity V_2, which ideally is in the axial direction.

V_b = tangential velocity of blade
V = absolute velocity of fluid
W = velocity of fluid relative to blade

© 1999 Encyclopædia Britannica, Inc.

Schematic of an impulse stage with velocity diagrams. Encyclopædia Britannica, Inc.

the steam to expand to a lower pressure while its velocity and kinetic energy increase. The steam is then directed to the moving passages or buckets where the kinetic energy is extracted. Since there is ideally no pressure drop and no acceleration in the blade passage, the magnitude of the velocity vector in the blades should remain constant. This also implies that the cross-sectional area normal to the flow remains constant, giving rise to the typical shape of a symmetrical impulse blade—namely, thick at the middle and sharp at the ends.

An important concept in impulse blading is velocities. Velocities are vectors that are added by the parallelogram law. The relative velocity of the fluid with reference to the blade at inlet (or exit) added vectorially to the (tangential) velocity of the blade must give the absolute velocity as seen by the stationary passages. That the kinetic energy at the nozzle exit (proportional to the square of the nozzle-leaving velocity) is much larger than that at the blade exit is apparent from the figure. In an ideal impulse stage, this change of kinetic energy is fully converted into useful work. For minimum exit kinetic energy in a symmetrical impulse blade, the rotor velocity should be about one-half of the entering steam velocity.

In an idealized reaction stage, about one-half of the enthalpy drop per stage is effected in the stator passage and the other half in the rotor passage. This implies that the pressure drop is also almost equal in both the stationary and the rotary passages, which tend to look like mirror images of each other. If the flow velocity is subsonic (below the velocity of sound in the fluid), an expanding passage flow will increase its velocity as the pressure drops while the cross-sectional area decreases simultaneously, thus leading to a curved nozzle shape.

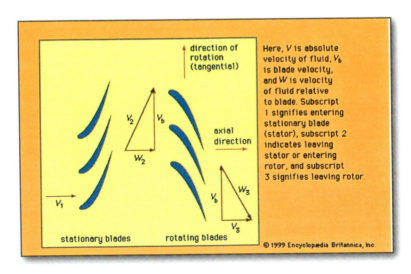

direction of rotation (tangential)

axial direction

Here, V is absolute velocity of fluid, V_b is blade velocity, and W is velocity of fluid relative to blade. Subscript 1 signifies entering stationary blade (stator), subscript 2 indicates leaving stator or entering rotor, and subscript 3 signifies leaving rotor.

V_2 V_b W_2 V_1 V_b W_3 V_3

stationary blades   rotating blades

© 1999 Encyclopædia Britannica, Inc.

An idealized 50-percent reaction stage for a steam turbine with velocity diagrams. Encyclopædia Britannica, Inc.

Since there is no pressure drop in an idealized impulse stage, pressure forces on the rotor play no role in this type of arrangement. By contrast, in a reaction stage, the effect of the changing pressure exerts a net force in the tangential direction (thus turning the wheel) and also in the axial direction. The latter tends to push the rotor into the ends of the casing, requiring a thrust bearing to absorb the axial load. In large turbines the axial load can be reduced by admitting the steam flow in the middle and expanding in both axial directions.

There is no need to match the increase of fluid velocity in the stator to that in the rotor (50-percent reaction). Other widely used combinations that fall between pure impulse and 50-percent reaction staging have been developed.

The large length of low-pressure blades imposes special requirements on stiffness in addition to aerodynamic shaping. The tangential velocity of the blade near the hub is much smaller than at the blade tip, while the axial through-flow velocity is maintained nearly constant. To match the flow, the blades must be twisted to have the correct approach angle for the incoming steam and at the same time avoid possible resonant vibrations.

TURBINE STAGING

Only a small fraction of the overall pressure drop available in a turbine can be extracted in a single stage consisting of a set of stationary nozzles or vanes and moving blades or buckets. In contrast to water turbines where the total head is extracted in a single runner, the steam velocities obtained from the enthalpy drop between steam generator and condenser would be prohibitively high. In addition, the volume increase of the expanding steam requires a large increase in the annular flow area to keep the axial through-flow velocity nearly constant. To this must be added limitations on blade length and blade-tip velocities to avoid excessive centrifugal stresses. In practice, the steam expansion is therefore broken up into many small segments or stages, each with a range of velocities and an appropriate blade size to permit efficient conversion of the thermal energy in the steam to mechanical energy. In modern turbines, three types of staging are employed, either separately or in combination: (1) pressure (or impulse) staging, (2) reaction staging, and (3) velocity-compound staging.

Pressure staging uses a number of sequential impulse stages similar to those mentioned above, except that the stationary passages also become highly curved nozzles. Pressure-staged turbines can range in power capacity from a few to more than 1.3 million kilowatts. Some manufacturers prefer to build units with impulse stages simply to reduce thrust-bearing loads. Such units may have as many as 20 sequential stages.

Reaction staging is similar to pressure staging, except that a greater number of reaction stages are required. The first turbine stage, however, is often an impulse stage for controlling the steam flow and for rapidly reducing the pressure in stationary nozzles from its high steam generator value, thereby lowering the pressure that the casing has to withstand. Reaction turbines require about twice as many stages as impulse-staged turbines for the same change in steam enthalpy. The cost and size of the turbines, however, are about the same because blading for pressure staging must withstand greater forces and must therefore be more rigidly constructed. Reaction turbines also have large axial thrust and require heavy-duty thrust bearings.

In velocity-compound staging a set of stationary nozzles is followed by two sets of moving blades with a stationary row of impulse blades between them to redirect the flow. Ideally this allows twice as much power to be extracted than from a single impulse stage for a given blade-tip velocity. It also permits a large pressure drop through the stationary nozzles. Velocity-compounding is well suited for small turbines, and is also sometimes used as the first stage in large turbines for control purposes. The inherent high steam velocities, however, tend to result in high losses and poor stage efficiencies.

POWER DEVELOPMENT

The theoretical maximum power produced by a turbine can be computed from the mass flow rate of the steam multiplied by the ideal enthalpy drop per unit mass between the steam generator exit and the condenser conditions. The actual power produced, however, is less because of friction, turbulence, leakage around the blade tips, and other losses. For the same maximum blade-tip velocity, pressure staging produces about twice as much ideal power per stage as reaction staging, while velocity-compound staging produces about four times as much.

The stage efficiency—i.e., the amount of work that is actually produced in each stage as compared to the maximum possible amount—can be higher for reaction stages than for impulse stages due to generally lower flow velocities and associated losses. The greater number of stages required, however, results in an overall turbine efficiency that is about the same for both. Efficient stages also require carefully designed seals along the rotor shaft and opposite the rotating blade tips to avoid leakage past the blades.

CHAPTER 5
CONVERTING
BIOMASS: BIOFUELS

Biofuel is any fuel derived from biomass—that is, plant material or animal waste. Since such feedstock material can be replenished readily, biofuel is considered to be a source of renewable energy, unlike fossil fuels such as petroleum, coal, and natural gas. Biofuel is perceived by its advocates as a cost-effective and environmentally benign alternative to petroleum and other fossil fuels, particularly within the context of rising petroleum prices and increased concern over the contributions made by fossil fuels to global warming. Many critics express concerns about the scope of the expansion of certain biofuels because of the economic and environmental costs associated with the refining process and the removal of vast areas of arable land from food production.

TYPES OF BIOFUELS

Some long-exploited biofuels, such as wood, can be used directly as a raw material that is burned to produce heat. The heat, in turn, can be used to run generators in a power plant to produce electricity. A number of existing power facilities burn grass, wood, or other kinds of biomass.

Liquid biofuels are of particular interest because of the vast infrastructure already in place to use them, especially for transportation. The liquid biofuel in greatest production is ethanol (ethyl alcohol), which is made by fermenting

"Gasohol," a blend of gasoline and ethanol, is an increasingly popular form of biofuel in the United States. Karen Bleier/AFP/Getty Images

starch or sugar. Brazil and the United States are among the leading producers of ethanol. In the United States, ethanol biofuel is made primarily from corn (maize) grain, and it is typically blended with gasoline to produce "gasohol," a fuel that is 10 percent ethanol. In Brazil, ethanol biofuel is made primarily from sugarcane, and it is commonly used as a 100-percent-ethanol fuel or in gasoline blends containing 85 percent ethanol.

The second most common liquid biofuel is biodiesel, which is made primarily from oily plants (such as the soybean or oil palm) and to a lesser extent from other oily sources (such as waste cooking fat from restaurant deep-frying). Biodiesel, which has found greatest acceptance in Europe, is used in diesel engines and usually blended with petroleum diesel fuel in various percentages.

Other biofuels include methane gas—which can be derived from the decomposition of biomass in the absence of oxygen—and methanol, butanol, and dimethyl ether—which are in development.

At present, much focus is on the development of methods to produce ethanol from biomass that possesses a high cellulose content. This cellulosic ethanol could be produced from abundant low-value material, including wood chips, grasses, crop residues, and municipal waste. The mix of commercially used biofuels will undoubtedly shift as these fuels are developed, but the range of possibilities presently known could furnish power for transportation, heating, cooling, and electricity.

THE MANUFACTURE OF ETHANOL

Ethanol is a member of a class of organic compounds that are given the general name alcohols; its molecular formula is C_2H_5OH. Ethyl alcohol is an important industrial

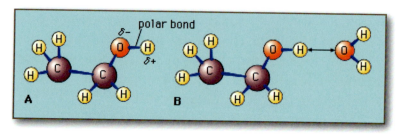

(A) The structure of ethanol. (B) The interaction between ethanol and water molecules. From S.S. Zumdahl, *Chemistry*, 3rd ed., copyright © 1993 by D.C. Heath and Company

chemical, used as a solvent and in the synthesis of other organic chemicals, in addition to being an additive to automotive gasoline to make gasohol. Ethyl alcohol is also the intoxicating ingredient of many alcoholic beverages such as beer, wine, and distilled spirits.

There are two main processes for the manufacture of ethyl alcohol. The fermentation of carbohydrates is the method used for making alcoholic beverages and also most of the ethanol used as biofuel. However, ethanol can also be produced by the hydration of ethylene, which in turn is obtained from petroleum. Fermentation involves the transformation of carbohydrates to ethyl alcohol by growing yeast cells. The chief raw materials fermented for the production of industrial alcohol are sugar crops such as beets and sugarcane and grain crops such as corn. Hydration of ethylene is achieved by passing a mixture of ethylene and a large excess of steam at high temperature and pressure over an acidic catalyst.

Ethyl alcohol produced either by fermentation or by synthesis is obtained as a dilute aqueous solution and must be concentrated by fractional distillation. Direct distillation can yield at best the constant-boiling-point mixture containing 95.6 percent by weight of ethyl alcohol.

Dehydration of the constant-boiling-point mixture yields anhydrous, or absolute, alcohol. Pure ethyl alcohol is a colourless, flammable liquid (boiling point 78.5 °C [173.3 °F]) with an agreeable ethereal odour and a burning taste.

ECONOMIC AND ENVIRONMENTAL CONSIDERATIONS

In evaluating the economic benefits of biofuels, the energy required to produce them has to be taken into account. For example, the process of growing corn to produce ethanol consumes fossil fuels in farming equipment, in fertilizer manufacturing, in corn transportation, and in ethanol distillation. In this respect ethanol made from corn represents a relatively small energy gain. The energy gain from sugarcane is greater, and that from cellulosic ethanol could be even greater.

Biofuels also supply environmental benefits but, depending on how they are manufactured, can also have serious environmental drawbacks. As a renewable energy source, plant-based biofuels in principle make little net contribution to global warming and climate change; the carbon dioxide (a major greenhouse gas) that enters the air during combustion will have been removed from the air earlier as growing plants engage in photosynthesis. Such a material is said to be "carbon neutral." In practice, however, the industrial production of agricultural biofuels can result in additional emissions of greenhouse gases that may offset the benefits of using a renewable fuel. These emissions include carbon dioxide from the burning of fossil fuels during the production process and nitrous oxide from soil that has been treated with nitrogen fertilizer. In this regard, cellulosic biomass is considered to be more beneficial.

Land use is also a major factor in evaluating the benefits of biofuels. Corn and soybeans are important foods, and their use in producing fuel can therefore affect the economics of food price and availability. By 2007 about one-fifth of the corn output in the United States was allocated to the production of biofuel, and one study showed that even if all U.S. corn land was used to produce ethanol, it could replace just 12 percent of gasoline consumption. In addition, crops grown for biofuel can compete for the world's natural habitats. For example, emphasis on ethanol derived from corn is shifting grasslands and brushlands to corn monocultures, and emphasis on biodiesel is bringing down ancient tropical forests to make way for palm plantations. Loss of natural habitat can change the hydrology, increase erosion, and generally reduce biodiversity of wildlife areas. The clearing of land can also result in the sudden release of a large amount of carbon dioxide as the plant matter that it contains is burned or allowed to decay.

Some of the disadvantages of biofuels apply mainly to low-diversity biofuel sources—corn, soybeans, sugarcane, oil palms—which are traditional agricultural crops. One alternative involves the use of highly diverse mixtures of species, with the North American tallgrass prairie as a specific example. Converting degraded agricultural land that is out of production to such high-diversity biofuel sources could increase wildlife area, reduce erosion, cleanse waterborne pollutants, store carbon dioxide from the air as carbon compounds in the soil, and ultimately restore fertility to degraded lands. Such biofuels could be burned directly to generate electricity or converted to liquid fuels as technologies develop.

The proper way to grow biofuels to serve all needs simultaneously will continue to be a matter of much experimentation and debate, but the fast growth in biofuel

Nebraska tallgrass prairie in bloom. The diverse vegetation that grows in North American tallgrass prairies may be a viable alternative to corn and sugarcane as a biofuel source. Joel Sartore/National Geographic Image Collection/Getty Images

production will likely continue. In the European Union, for example, biofuels are planned to account for 5.75 percent of transport fuels by 2010, and 10 percent of European vehicles are expected to run exclusively on biofuels by 2020. In the United States the Energy Independence and Security Act of 2007 mandated the use of 136 billion litres (36 billion gallons) of biofuels annually by 2020, more than a sixfold increase over 2006 production levels. The legislation also requires, with certain stipulations, that 79 billion litres (21 billion gallons) of the total amount be biofuels other than corn-derived ethanol, and it continued certain government subsidies and tax incentives for biofuel production. In addition, the technology for producing cellulosic ethanol is being developed at a number of pilot plants in the United States.

NEW FINDINGS ON BIOFUELS

A study published by the Nature Conservancy in February 2008 found that biofuel production, which was seen as a way of reducing the accumulation of carbon dioxide in the atmosphere, was likely to have the opposite effect when biofuel crops were grown on land converted from other uses. According to the study, the conversion of rainforest, peatland, savanna, or other grassland to biofuel production in Brazil, Southeast Asia, and the United States released up to 420 times more carbon dioxide than the reduction in emissions achieved by using biofuels instead of fossil fuels. Another study, by the German Marshall Fund of the United States, found that when land-use change was taken into account, the development of corn-based ethanol production would double greenhouse-gas emissions over 30 years.

One distinctive promise of biofuels is that, in combination with an emerging technology called carbon capture and storage, the process of producing and using biofuels may be capable of perpetually removing carbon dioxide from the atmosphere. Under this vision, biofuel crops would remove carbon dioxide from the air as they grow, and energy facilities would capture the carbon dioxide given off as biofuels are burned to generate power. Captured carbon dioxide could be sequestered (stored) in long-term repositories such as geologic formations beneath the land, in sediments of the deep ocean, or conceivably as solids such as carbonates.

CHAPTER 6
SPLITTING
THE ATOM:
NUCLEAR ENERGY

Nuclear energy, or atomic energy, is energy that is released in significant amounts in processes that affect atomic nuclei, the dense cores of atoms. It is distinct from the energy of other atomic phenomena such as ordinary chemical reactions, which involve only the orbital electrons of atoms. One method of releasing nuclear energy is by controlled nuclear fission in nuclear reactors, which are operated in many parts of the world as research tools, as systems for producing radioisotopes, and most prominently as energy sources. The latter are commonly called power reactors.

NUCLEAR FISSION

Fission is the process in which a heavy nucleus splits into two smaller fragments. A large amount of energy is released in this process, and this energy is the basis of nuclear power systems. The nuclear fragments are in very excited states and emit neutrons and other forms of radiation. The neutrons can then cause new fissions, which in turn yield more neutrons, and so forth. Such a continuous self-sustaining series of fissions constitutes a fission chain reaction.

In an atomic bomb the chain reaction is designed to increase in intensity until much of the material has fissioned. This increase is very rapid and produces the extremely sharp, tremendously energetic explosions

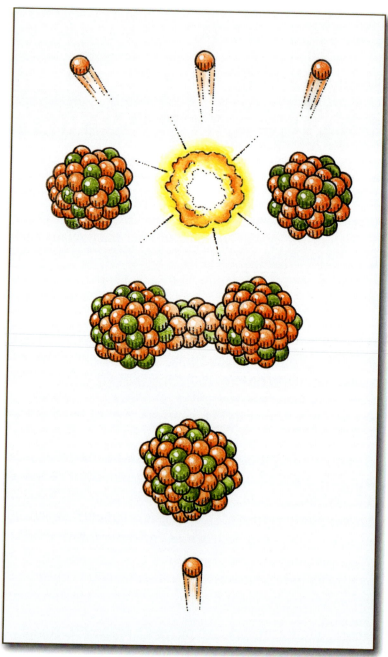

An illustration depicting nuclear fission, wherein a neutron splits a heavy nucleus and releases energy. Dorling Kindersley/Getty Images

characteristic of such bombs. In a nuclear reactor the chain reaction is maintained at a controlled, nearly constant level. Nuclear reactors are so designed that they cannot explode like atomic bombs.

Most of the energy of fission—about 85 percent of it—is released within a very short time after the process occurs. The rest of the energy comes from the radioactive decay of fission products, which is what the fragments are called after they have emitted neutrons. Radioactive decay continues when the fission chain has been stopped, and its energy must be dealt with in any proper reactor design.

CHAIN REACTION AND CRITICALITY

The course of a chain reaction is determined by the probability that a neutron released in fission will cause a subsequent fission. If on the average less than one neutron causes another fission, the rate of fission will decrease with time and ultimately drop to zero. This situation is said to be subcritical. When an average of one neutron from a fission causes another fission, the fission rate is steady and the reactor is critical. A critical reactor is what is usually desired. When more than one neutron causes a subsequent fission, fission rate and power increase and the situation is termed supercritical. In order to be able to increase power, reactors are designed to be slightly supercritical when all controls are removed.

REACTOR CONTROL

A parameter called reactivity is positive when a reactor is supercritical, zero at criticality, and negative when the reactor is subcritical. Reactivity can be controlled by adding or removing fuel, changing the fraction of neutrons that leaks from the system, or changing the amount of an absorber that competes with the fuel for neutrons. Control is generally accomplished by varying absorbers, which are commonly in the form of movable elements—control rods—or sometimes by changing the concentration of the absorber in a reactor coolant. Leakage changes are usually automatic; for example, an increase of power may cause coolant to boil, which in turn increases neutron leakage and reduces reactivity. This, and other types of negative power-reactivity feedbacks, are vital aspects of safe reactor design.

Reactor control is facilitated by the presence of delayed neutrons. These neutrons are emitted by fission products some time after fission has occurred. The fraction of delayed neutrons is small, but there is a sufficient number of such neutrons for the types of changes needed to regulate an operating reactor, and so the chain reaction must "wait" for them before it can respond. This eases operation considerably.

FISSILE AND FERTILE MATERIALS

All heavy nuclides can fission if they are in an excited enough state, but only a few fission readily when struck by slow (low-energy) neutrons. Such species of atoms are called fissile. The most important of these are uranium-233 (^{233}U), uranium-235 (^{235}U), plutonium-239 (^{239}Pu), and plutonium-241 (^{241}Pu). The only one that occurs in usable amounts in nature is uranium-235, which makes up a mere 0.711 percent of natural uranium by weight. Uranium-233 can be produced by neutron capture in natural thorium (^{232}Th); that is to say, when a nucleus of thorium-232 absorbs a neutron, it becomes uranium-233. Similarly, plutonium-239 is created by neutron capture in uranium-238 (^{238}U; the principal constituent of naturally occurring uranium), and plutonium-241 is formed when a neutron is absorbed into plutonium-240 (^{240}Pu). Plutonium-240 builds up over time in most power reactors. Thorium-232, uranium-238, and plutonium-240 are termed fertile materials because they can be transformed into fissile materials.

A power reactor contains both fissile and fertile materials. The fertile materials replace fissile materials that are destroyed by fission. This permits the reactor to run longer before the amount of fissile material decreases to the point where criticality can no longer be maintained.

HEAT REMOVAL

The energy of fission is quickly converted to heat, the bulk of which is deposited in the fuel. A coolant is therefore required to remove this heat. The most common coolant is water, but any fluid can be used. Heavy water (deuterium oxide), air, carbon dioxide, helium, liquid sodium, sodium-potassium alloy (called NaK), molten salts, and hydrocarbons have all been used in reactors or reactor experiments. Some research reactors are operated at very low power and have no need for a dedicated cooling system; in such units the small amount of heat that is generated is removed by conduction and convection to the environment. Very high power reactors must have extremely sophisticated cooling systems to remove heat quickly and reliably; otherwise, the heat will build up in the reactor fuel and melt it.

SHIELDING

An operating reactor is a powerful source of radiation, since fission and subsequent radioactive decay produce neutrons and gamma rays, both of which are highly penetrating radiations. A reactor must have special shielding around it to absorb this radiation in order to protect technicians and other reactor personnel.

Workers inside a massive reactor thermo shield of the U.S. Hinkley Point nuclear power station in the 1950s. Shields are the first line of defense against accidental radiation leakage. Chris Ware/Hulton Archive/Getty Images

In a popular class of research reactors known as "swimming pools," shielding is provided by placing the reactor in a large, deep pool of water. In other kinds of reactors, the shield consists of a thick concrete structure around the reactor system. The shield also may contain heavy metals, such as lead or steel, for more effective absorption of gamma rays, and heavy aggregates may be used in the concrete itself for the same purpose.

CRITICAL CONCENTRATION AND SIZE

Not every arrangement of material containing fissile fuel can be brought to criticality. Even if there were no leakage of neutrons from a reactor, a critical concentration of fissile material must be present. Otherwise, absorption of neutrons by other constituents of the reactor will be too high to permit a critical chain reaction to proceed. Similarly, even if there is a high enough concentration for criticality, the reactor must be large enough so that not too many neutrons leak out before being absorbed. This imposes a critical size limit on a reactor of a given concentration.

Although the only useful fissile material in nature, uranium-235, is found in natural uranium, there are just a few combinations and arrangements of this and other materials that can be brought to criticality. To increase the range of feasible reactor designs, enriched uranium can be used. Most of today's power reactors employ enriched uranium fuel in which the percentage of uranium-235 has been increased to 3 to 4 percent. This is about five times the concentration in natural uranium.

THERMAL, INTERMEDIATE, AND FAST REACTORS

Reactors are conveniently classified according to the typical energies of the neutrons that cause fission. Neutrons emanating in fission are very energetic; their average energy is around two million electron volts (MeV), 80 million times higher than the energy of atoms in ordinary matter at room temperature. As the neutrons collide with nuclei in a reactor, they lose energy. The choice of reactor materials and of fissile material concentrations determines how much they are slowed down by these collisions before causing fission.

In a thermal reactor, enough collisions are permitted to occur so that most of the neutrons reach thermal equilibrium with the atoms of the reactor at energies of a few hundredths of an electron volt. Neutrons lose energy most efficiently by colliding with light atoms such as hydrogen (mass 1), deuterium (mass 2), beryllium (mass 9), and carbon (mass 12). Materials that contain atoms of this kind—water, heavy water, beryllium metal and oxide, and graphite—are deliberately incorporated into the reactor for this reason and are known as moderators. Since water and heavy water also can function as coolants, they can do double duty in thermal reactors.

THE INTERNATIONAL ATOMIC ENERGY AGENCY

The IAEA is an autonomous intergovernmental organization dedicated to increasing the contribution of atomic energy to the world's peace and well-being and ensuring that agency assistance is not used for military purposes. The IAEA and its director general, Mohamed ElBaradei, won the Nobel Prize for Peace in 2005.

The agency was established by representatives of more than 80 countries in October 1956, nearly three years after U.S. Pres. Dwight D. Eisenhower's "Atoms for Peace" speech to the United Nations General Assembly, in which Eisenhower called for the creation of an international organization for monitoring the diffusion of nuclear resources and technology. The IAEA's statute officially came into force on July 29, 1957. Its activities include research on the applications of atomic energy to medicine, agriculture, water resources, and industry; the operation of conferences, training programs, fellowships, and publications to promote the exchange of technical information and skills; the provision of technical assistance, especially to less-developed countries; and the establishment and administration of radiation safeguards. As part of the Treaty on the Non-Proliferation of Nuclear Weapons (1968), all non-nuclear powers are required to negotiate a safeguards agreement with the IAEA; as part of that agreement, the IAEA is given authority to monitor nuclear programs and to inspect nuclear facilities.

The General Conference, consisting of all members (in the early 21st century some 135 countries were members), meets annually to approve the budget and programs and to debate the IAEA's general policies; it also is responsible for approving the appointment of a director general and admitting new members. The Board of Governors, which consists of 35 members who meet about five times per year, is charged with carrying out the agency's statutory functions, approving safeguards agreements, and appointing the director general. The day-to-day affairs of the IAEA are run by the Secretariat, which is headed by the director general, who is assisted by six deputies; the Secretariat's departments include nuclear energy, nuclear safety, nuclear sciences and application, safeguards, and technical cooperation. Headquarters are in Vienna.

One disadvantage of thermal reactors is that at low energies uranium-235 and plutonium-239 not only can be fissioned by thermal (or slow) neutrons but also can capture neutrons without undergoing fission. This destroys fissile atoms without any fission to show for it. When neutrons of higher energy cause fission, fewer of these captures occur. To achieve this, a reactor can be built to operate without a moderator. Then, depending on how many collisions take place with heavier atoms before fission occurs, the typical fission-causing neutrons can have energies in the range of 0.5 electron volt to thousands of electron volts (intermediate reactors) or several hundred thousand electron volts (fast reactors). Such reactors require higher concentrations of fissile material to reach criticality than do thermal reactors but are more efficient at converting fertile material to fissile material. Indeed, they can be designed to produce more than one new fissile atom for each fissile atom destroyed. Such reactors are called breeders. Breeder reactors may become particularly important if the world demand for nuclear power turns out to be a long-term one, since their fuel is manufactured from very abundant fertile materials.

CHAPTER 7
NUCLEAR REACTOR DESIGN AND COMPONENTS

There are many ways in which a reactor may be designed and constructed. Several types have been experimentally realized. Over the years, nuclear engineers have developed reactors with solid fuels and liquid fuels, thick reflectors and no reflectors, forced cooling circuits and natural conduction or convection heat-removal systems, and so on. Most reactors, however, have certain basic components, which are described in this chapter.

CORE

All reactors have a core, a central region that contains the fuel, fuel cladding, coolant, and, where separate from the latter, moderator. It is in the core that fission occurs and the resulting neutrons migrate.

The fuel is usually heterogeneous—i.e., it consists of elements containing fissile material along with a diluent. This diluting agent may be fertile material or simply material that has good mechanical and chemical properties and that does not readily absorb neutrons. The diluted fissile material is enclosed in a cladding—a substance that isolates the fuel from the coolant and keeps the radioactive fission products contained.

FUEL TYPES

Different kinds of reactors use different types of fuel elements. For example, the light-water reactor (LWR), which is

The installation of a reactor core at a Taiwanese nuclear power plant. As the place where nuclear fission takes place, the core is an essential component of a nuclear reactor. Patrick Lin/AFP/Getty Images

the most widely used variety for commercial power generation in the United States, employs a fuel consisting of pellets of sintered uranium dioxide loaded into cladding tubes of zirconium alloy that measure about one centimetre (.4 inch) in diameter and roughly three to four metres (9.8 to 13.1 feet) long. These tubes, called pins, are bundled together into a fuel assembly, with the pins arranged in a square lattice. The uranium used in the fuel is 3- to 4-percent enriched. Since light (ordinary) water tends to absorb more neutrons than do other moderators, such enrichment is crucial. The CANDU (Canadian deuterium-uranium) reactor, which is the principal type of heavy-water reactor, uses natural uranium compacted into pellets. These pellets are inserted in tubes arranged in a lattice. Such a fuel assembly measures about one metre (3.3 feet) in length, and several assemblies are arranged end-to-end within a channel inside the reactor core.

In a high-temperature graphite reactor the fuel is made of small spherical particles containing uranium dioxide at the centre with concentric shells of carbon, silicon carbide, and carbon around them. (These shells serve as microscopic cladding.) The particles are mixed with graphite and encased in a macroscopic graphite cladding. In a sodium-cooled fast reactor, commonly called a liquid-metal reactor (LMR), the fuel consists of dioxide pellets (French design) or uranium-plutonium-zirconium metal alloy pins (U.S. design) in steel cladding.

The most common type of fuel used in research reactors consists of plates of a uranium-aluminum alloy with an aluminum cladding. The uranium is enriched to 20 percent, and silicon, along with aluminum, are included in the "meat" of the plate. A common variety of research reactor, known as TRIGA (from training, research, and isotope-production reactors–General Atomic), employs a fuel of mixed uranium and zirconium hydride in zirconium cladding.

COOLANTS AND MODERATORS

A variety of substances, including light water, heavy water, air, carbon dioxide, helium, liquid sodium, liquid sodium-potassium alloy, and hydrocarbons (oils), have been used as coolants. Such substances are good conductors of heat and serve to carry the thermal energy produced by fission from the core to the steam-generating equipment of the nuclear power plant.

In many cases, the same substance functions as both coolant and moderator, as in the case of light and heavy water. The moderator slows down the fast (high-energy) neutrons emitted in fission to speeds at which they are more likely to induce fission. In doing so, the moderator helps initiate and sustain a fission chain reaction.

REFLECTOR

A reflector is a region of unfueled material surrounding the core. Its function is to scatter neutrons that leak from the core and thereby return some of them to the core. This reduces core size and smooths out the power density. The reflector is particularly important in research reactors, since it is the region in which much of the experimental apparatus is located. Some reflectors are located inside the core as central islands in which high neutron intensities can be achieved for experimental purposes. In most types of power reactors, a reflector is less important, because the reactors are large and do not leak many neutrons. Yet, as it serves to keep the power density uniform, such an unfueled zone of moderator material is left around the core.

The liquid-metal reactor represents a special case. Most sodium-cooled reactors are deliberately built to allow a large fraction of their neutrons—those not needed to maintain the chain reaction—to leak from the core. These neutrons are valuable because they can produce new fissile material if they are absorbed by fertile material. Thus, fertile material—generally depleted uranium or its dioxide—is placed around the core to catch the leaking neutrons. Such an absorbing reflector is referred to as a blanket or a breeding blanket.

REACTOR CONTROL ELEMENTS

All reactors need special elements for control. Although control can be achieved by varying parameters of the coolant circuit or by varying the amount of absorber dissolved in the coolant or moderator, by far the most common method involves the use of special absorbing assemblies—namely, control rods or sometimes blades.

Typically a reactor is equipped with three types of rods for different purposes: (1) safety rods for starting up and shutting down the reactor, (2) regulating rods for adjusting the reactor's power rate, and (3) shim rods for compensating for changes in reactivity as fuel is depleted by fission and capture.

The most important function of the safety rods is to shut down the reactor, either when such a shutdown is scheduled or in case of a real or suspected emergency. These rods contain enough absorber to terminate a chain reaction under any conceivable condition. They are withdrawn before fuel is loaded and remain available in case a loading error requires their action. After the fuel is loaded, the rods are inserted, to be withdrawn again when the reactor is ready for operation. The mechanism by which they are moved is designed to be fail-safe in the sense

A scrum valve for emergency control rods at the Hamaoka nuclear power station in Omaezaki City, Japan. Installed as a safety measure, rods can stop a reactor in case of emergency. Bloomberg via Getty Images

that if there is a mechanical failure the safety rods will fall by gravity into the reactor. In some cases, moreover, the safety rods have an automatic feature, such as a fuse, which releases them by virtue of physical effects independent of electronic signals.

Regulating rods are deliberately designed to affect reactivity only by a small degree. It is assumed that at some time the rods might be totally withdrawn by mistake, and the idea is to keep the added reactivity in such cases well within sensible limits. A well-designed regulating rod will add so little reactivity when it is removed that the delayed neutrons will continue to control the rate of power increase.

Shim rods are designed to compensate for the effects of burnup (i.e., energy production). Reactivity changes resulting from burnup can be large, but they occur slowly over periods of days to years, as compared to the seconds-to-minutes range over which safety actions and routine regulation take place. Therefore, shim rods may control a significant amount of reactivity, but they will work perfectly well under constraints on their speed of movement. A common way in which shims are operated is by inserting or removing them as regulating rods reach the end of their most useful position range. When this happens, shim rods are moved so that the regulating rods can be reset.

The functions of shim and safety rods are sometimes combined in rods that have low rates of withdrawal but that can be rapidly inserted. This is usually done when the effect of burnup is to decrease reactivity. The rods are only partially inserted at the outset of operation, but the reactor can be quickly shut down by lowering them all the way into the core (scramming). As operation proceeds, the rods are moved farther out so that there is a greater shutdown reactivity margin.

The amount of shim control required can be reduced by the use of a burnable "poison." This is a neutron-absorbing material, such as boron or gadolinium, which will burn off faster than the fissile material does. At the beginning of operation, this controls the extra reactivity that has been built into the fuel to compensate for the amount of fuel consumed. At the end of an operating period, the absorber material will have been almost completely destroyed by neutron capture.

STRUCTURAL COMPONENTS

These are the parts of a reactor system that hold the reactor together and permit it to function as a useful energy source. The most important structural component is usually the reactor vessel. In both the light-water reactor and the high-temperature gas-controlled reactor (HTGR), a pressure vessel is used so that the coolant can be contained and operated under conditions appropriate for power generation—namely, high temperature and pressure. Within the reactor vessel are structural grids for holding the reactor core and solid reflectors, coolant channels, control-rod guide channels, internal thermohydraulic components (e.g., pumps or steam circulators) in some cases, instrument tubes, and parts of safety systems.

COOLANT SYSTEM

The function of a power reactor installation is to extract the heat of nuclear fission and convert it to useful power, generally electricity. The coolant system plays a pivotal role in performing this function. A coolant fluid enters the core at low temperature and leaves it at higher temperature. This higher temperature fluid is then directed to conventional thermodynamic components where the heat is converted into electrical power. In most light-water, heavy-water, and gas-cooled power reactors, the coolant is maintained at high pressure. Sodium and organic coolants operate at atmospheric pressure.

Research reactors have very simple heat removal systems in which coolant is run through the reactor and the heat that is removed is transferred to ambient air or to water without going through a power cycle. In research reactors of the lowest power running at only a few kilowatts, this may involve simple heat exchange to tap water or to a pool of water cooled with ambient air. During operation at higher power levels, the heat is usually removed by means of a small natural-draft cooling tower.

CONTAINMENT SYSTEM

Reactors are designed with the expectation that they will operate safely without releasing radioactivity to their surroundings. It is, however, recognized that accidents can occur. An approach using multiple barriers has been adopted to deal with such accidents. These barriers are, successively, the fuel cladding, primary vessel, and thick shielding. As a final barrier, the reactor is housed in a containment structure. This consists basically of the reactor building, which is designed and tested to prevent any radioactivity that escapes from the reactor from being released to the environment.

The containment structure must be at least nominally airtight. In practice, it must be able to maintain its integrity under circumstances of a drastic nature, such as accidents in which most of the contents of the reactor core are released to the building. It has to withstand pressure buildups and damage from debris propelled by an explosion within the reactor, and it must pass a test to demonstrate that it will not leak more than a small

Workers inspect the dome and walls of a reactor containment building at the Clinton Power Station in Illinois. Bloomberg via Getty Images

fraction of its contents over a period of several days, even when its internal pressure is well above that of the surrounding air.

The most common form of containment building is a cylindrical structure with a spherical dome, which is characteristic of LWR systems. This is much more typical of nuclear plants than the large cooling tower that is often used as a symbol for nuclear power. (It should be noted that cooling towers are found at large modern coal- and oil-fired power stations as well.) Reactors other than those of the LWR type also have containment structures, but they vary in shape and construction. When it can be justified that major pressure buildups are not to be expected, the containment can be any form of airtight structure.

In the United States, containment structures are required for all commercial power reactors and all high-power research reactors. In general, low-power research reactors are exempt, based on the common assumption that an accident in such systems will not lead to a widespread release of radioactivity. Reactors operated by the U.S. Department of Energy and by the armed services also are exempt, a matter which has caused considerable controversy. Some of these have containment structures, while others do not.

The concept of containment originated in the United States during the 1950s and has been generally accepted throughout much of the world. The Soviet bloc countries, however, did not concur with this view, and when containment was provided it was generally not up to Western standards. For example, Chernobyl Unit 4, which suffered a catastrophic explosive accident and fire in 1986, merely had an internal structure that could only withstand the loss of function of a single pressure tube. Though called containment, this was a misnomer by Western standards.

The most severe test of a containment system occurred during an accident in the United States in 1979 at Three Mile Island Unit 2, near Harrisburg, Pa. In this installation, a stoppage of core cooling resulted in the destruction, including partial melting, of the entire core and the release of a large part of its radioactivity to the enclosure around the reactor. In spite of a hydrogen deflagration that also occurred during the accident, the containment structure prevented all but a very small amount of radioactivity from entering the environment and must be credited with having prevented a major radioactive release and its consequences.

TYPES OF REACTORS

Most of the world's existing reactors are power reactors. There also are many research reactors, and the navies of many nations include submarines and surface ships driven by propulsion reactors. There are several types of power reactors, but only one, the light-water reactor, is widely used. Accordingly, this variety is discussed in considerable detail here. Other significant types are briefly described, as are research and propulsion reactors.

LIGHT-WATER REACTOR

As noted above, LWRs are power reactors that are cooled and moderated with ordinary water. There are two basic types: the pressurized-water reactor (PWR) and the boiling-water reactor (BWR). In the first type, high-pressure, high-temperature water removes heat from the core and is then passed to a steam generator. Here the heat of the coolant is transferred to a stream of water in the generator, causing the water to boil and slightly superheat. The steam generated by this serves as the working fluid in a steam-turbine cycle.

In a boiling-water reactor, water passing through the core is allowed to boil at intermediate pressure, and the steam from the reactor is used directly in the power cycle. Although the BWR seems simpler, the PWR has advantages with regard to fuel utilization and power density, and the two concepts have been economically competitive with each other since the 1960s. Both these light-water reactors are fueled with uranium dioxide pellets in zirconium alloy cladding. The BWR fuel is slightly less enriched, but the PWR fuel produces more energy before being discharged, and so these two aspects balance each other out economically. Because the BWR operates at lower pressure, it has a thinner pressure vessel than the PWR; however, because its power density is somewhat lower, the BWR's vessel has a larger diameter for the same reactor power. The internal system of a BWR is more complex, since there are internal recirculation pumps and complex steam separation and drying equipment within its vessel. Though the internals of the PWR are simpler, a BWR power plant is smaller because it has no steam generators. In fact, the steam generators—there are usually four of them in a big PWR plant—are larger than the reactor vessel itself. The control rods of a typical PWR are inserted from the top (through the reactor head), while those of a BWR are inserted from the bottom.

Light-water reactors are refueled by removing the reactor head—after lowering and unlatching the safety rods in the case of a PWR. This exposes the reactor to visual observation. The pressure vessel is filled to the top with water, and, since the core is near the bottom of the vessel, the water acts as a shield for this operation. Then, the fuel assemblies to be removed are lifted up into a shielded cask within which they are transferred to a storage pool for cooling while they are still highly radioactive. Many of the remaining assemblies are then shifted within the core, and finally fresh fuel is loaded into the empty fuel positions. The purpose of shifting fuel at the time of reload is to achieve an optimal reactivity and power distribution for the next cycle of operation. Reloading is a time-consuming operation. In principle, it could be accomplished in three weeks, but in practice the plant undergoes maintenance during reload, which can take considerably more time—up to a few months. Utilities schedule maintenance and reload during the spring and fall when electricity demand is lowest and the system usually has reserve capacity.

The discharged fuel stored in the storage pool is not only highly radioactive but also continues to produce energy. This energy is removed by natural circulation of the water in the storage pool. Originally it was expected that this spent fuel could be shipped out for reprocessing within two years, but this option is currently practiced only in France. In the United States, storage pools have continued to receive spent fuel, and some of the pools are filling up. Options available to nuclear plant operators are to store the spent fuel more densely than originally planned, to build new pools, or to store the oldest, no longer very hot fuel in above-ground silos (dry storage). Ultimately this fuel will be transferred to the U.S. Department of Energy for reprocessing or waste disposal or both, though a viable disposal program has not been established.

During the 1970s light-water reactors represented the cheapest source of new electricity in most parts of the world, and it still is economical in Japan, Korea, Taiwan, and France and many other European countries. In the United States, however, strict regulation of light-water reactors during the 1980s, coupled with a decrease in reactor research and development activity, have made the competitive nature of new light-water reactor installations problematic. Plants that have been exceptionally well managed during construction and operation remain competitive; unfortunately, these are not the rule. New designs, developed abroad, may alter this situation, however.

HIGH-TEMPERATURE GAS-COOLED REACTOR

The HTGR, as mentioned above, is fueled with a mixture of graphite and fuel-bearing microspheres. There are two competitive designs of this reactor type: (1) a German system that uses spherical fuel elements of tennis-ball size loaded into a graphite silo and (2) an American version in which the fuel is loaded into precisely located graphite hexagonal prisms. In both variants, the coolant consists of helium pressurized to about 100 bars. In the German system the helium passes through interstices in the bed of the spherical fuel elements, while in the American system it passes through holes in the graphite prisms. Both are capable of operating at very high temperature, since graphite has an extremely high sublimation temperature and helium is completely inert chemically. The hot helium can be used directly as the working fluid in a high-temperature gas turbine, or its heat can be utilized to generate steam for a water cycle. Experimental prototypes of both the American and German designs have been built, but no commercial plants are on order.

LIQUID-METAL REACTORS

Sodium-cooled, fast-neutron-spectrum reactors received much attention during the 1960s and '70s when it appeared that their breeding capabilities would soon be needed to supply fissile material to a rapidly expanding nuclear industry. When it became clear in the 1980s that this was not a realistic expectation, enthusiasm slackened. The developmental work of the previous decades, however, resulted in the construction of a number of liquid-metal reactors around the world—in the United States, the former Soviet Union, France, Britain, Japan, and Germany.

Most liquid-metal reactors are fueled with uranium dioxide or mixed uranium–plutonium dioxides. In the United States, however, the greatest success has been with metal fuels. While some liquid-metal reactors are of the loop type, equipped with heat exchangers and pumps outside the primary reactor vessel, others are of the pool variety, featuring a large volume of primary sodium in a pool that also contains the primary pumps and primary-to-secondary heat exchanger. In all types, the heat extracted from the core by primary sodium is transferred to a secondary, nonradioactive sodium loop, which serves as the heat source for a steam generator and turbine. The pool type seems to have some advantage in terms of safety in that the large volume of primary sodium heats up only slowly even if no power is extracted; thus, the reactor is effectively isolated from upsets in the balance of the plant. The reactor core in all such systems is a tightly packed bundle of fuel in steel cladding through which the sodium coolant flows to extract the heat. Most liquid-metal reactors are breeders or are capable of breeding, which is to say that they all produce more fissile material than they consume.

CANDU REACTOR

Canada focused its developmental efforts on reactors that would utilize abundant domestic natural uranium as fuel without having to resort to enrichment services that could be supplied only by other countries. The result of this policy was CANDU—the line of natural uranium-fueled reactors moderated and cooled by heavy water. A reactor of this kind consists of a tank, or calandria vessel, containing cold heavy water at normal pressure. The calandria is pierced by pressure tubes made of zirconium alloy, in which the natural uranium fuel is placed and the heavy water coolant is circulated. Power is obtained by transferring the heat from the exiting hot pressurized heavy water to a steam generator and then running the steam from the latter through a conventional turbine cycle.

The fuel assembly of a CANDU reactor, which consists of a bundle of short zirconium alloy-clad tubes containing natural uranium dioxide pellets, can be changed while the system is running. A new assembly is simply pushed into one end of a pressure tube and the old one collected as it drops out at the other end. This feature has given the CANDU higher capacity factors than other reactor types. Several countries have purchased CANDU reactors for the same reason that they were developed by Canada—to be independent of imported enrichment services.

ADVANCED GAS-COOLED REACTOR

The advanced gas-cooled reactor (AGR) was developed in Britain as the successor to reactors of the Calder Hall class, which combined plutonium production and power generation. Calder Hall was the first nuclear station to feed an appreciable amount of power into a civilian network. It was fueled with slugs of natural uranium metal canned in aluminum, cooled with carbon dioxide, and employed a moderator consisting of a block of graphite pierced by fuel channels. In the advanced gas-cooled reactor, fuel pins clad in Zircaloy (trademark for alloys of zirconium having low percentages of chromium, nickel, iron, and tin) and loaded with 2-percent enriched uranium dioxide are placed into zirconium-alloy channels that pierce a graphite moderator block. The enriched fuel permits operation to economic levels of fuel burnup. A coolant of carbon dioxide transports heat to a steam generator, activating a steam-turbine cycle. Although a number of advanced gas-cooled reactors have been built in Britain, they have been less trouble-free and more costly than expected, and no new ones are planned.

OTHER POWER REACTOR TYPES

A large variety of reactor types have been built and operated on an experimental basis. One example is organic liquid-cooled and -moderated reactors that operate like a pressurized-water reactor without requiring high pressures in the primary circuit. Other examples include sodium-cooled, graphite-moderated reactors and heavy-water reactors built in a pressure-vessel design.

CHAPTER 8
FUEL CELLS

Fuel cells are devices that convert the chemical energy of a fuel directly into electricity by electrochemical reactions. A fuel cell resembles a battery in many respects, but it can supply electrical energy over a much longer period of time. This is because a fuel cell is continuously supplied with fuel and air (or oxygen) from an external source, whereas a battery contains only a limited amount of fuel material and oxidant that are depleted with use. For this reason fuel cells have been used for decades in space probes, satellites, and manned spacecraft.

Around the world thousands of stationary fuel cell systems have been installed in utility power plants, hospitals, schools, hotels, and office buildings for both primary and backup power. Many waste-treatment plants use fuel cell technology to generate power from the methane gas produced by decomposing garbage. Numerous municipalities in Japan, Europe, and the United States lease fuel cell vehicles for public transportation and for use by service personnel. Personal fuel cell vehicles were first sold in Germany in 2004.

The United States government and several state governments, most notably California, have launched programs to encourage the development and use of hydrogen fuel cells in transportation and other applications. While the technology has proven to be workable, efforts to make it commercially competitive have been less successful because of concern with the explosive power of hydrogen, the relatively low energy density of hydrogen, and the high cost of platinum catalysts used to create an electric current by separating electrons from hydrogen atoms.

PRINCIPLES OF OPERATION

A fuel cell (actually a group of cells) has essentially the same kinds of components as a battery. As in the latter, each cell of a fuel cell system has a matching pair of electrodes. These are the anode, which supplies electrons, and the cathode, which absorbs electrons. Both electrodes must be immersed in and separated by an electrolyte, which may be a liquid or a solid but which must, in either case,

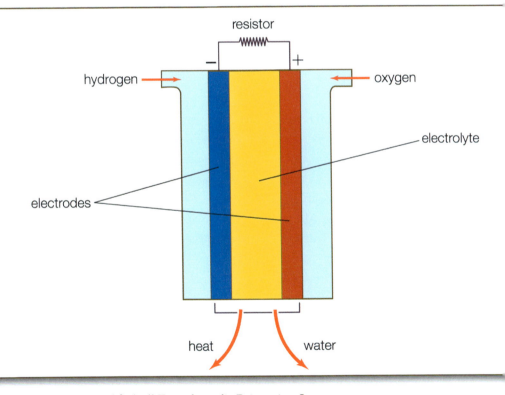

A typical fuel cell. Encyclopædia Britannica, Inc.

conduct ions between the electrodes in order to complete the chemistry of the system. A fuel, such as hydrogen, is supplied to the anode, where it is oxidized, producing hydrogen ions and electrons. An oxidizer, such as oxygen, is supplied to the cathode, where the hydrogen ions from the anode absorb electrons from the latter and react with the oxygen to produce water.

The difference between the respective energy levels at the electrodes (electromotive force) is the voltage per unit cell. The amount of electric current available to the external circuit depends on the chemical activity and amount of the substances supplied as fuels. The current-producing process continues for as long as there is a supply of reactants, for the electrodes and electrolyte of a fuel cell, unlike those in a regular battery, are designed to remain unchanged by chemical reaction.

THE ELECTROCHEMICAL SYSTEM

A practical fuel cell is necessarily a complex system. It must have features to boost the activity of the fuel, pumps and blowers, fuel-storage containers, and a variety of sophisticated sensors and controls with which to monitor and adjust the operation of the system. The operating capability and lifetime of each of these system design features may limit the performance of the fuel cell.

As in the case of other electrochemical systems, fuel cell operation is dependent on temperature. The chemical activity of the fuels and the value of the activity promoters, or catalysts, are reduced by low temperatures (e.g., 0 °C, or 32 °F). Very high temperatures, on the other hand, improve the activity factors but may reduce the functioning lifetime of the electrodes, blowers, construction materials, and sensors. Each type of fuel cell thus has an operating-temperature design range, and a significant departure from this range is likely to diminish both capacity and lifetime.

A fuel cell, like a battery, is inherently a high-efficiency device. Unlike internal-combustion machines, in which a fuel is burned and gas is expanded to do work, the fuel cell converts chemical energy directly into electrical energy. Because of this fundamental characteristic, fuel cells may convert fuels to useful energy at an efficiency as high as 60 percent, whereas the internal-combustion engine is limited to efficiencies near 40 percent or less. The high efficiency means that much less fuel and a smaller storage container are needed for a fixed energy requirement. For this reason, fuel cells are an attractive power supply for space missions of limited duration and for other situations where fuel is very expensive and difficult to supply. They also emit no noxious gases such as nitrogen dioxide and produce virtually no noise during operation, making them contenders for local municipal power-generation stations.

A fuel cell can be designed to operate reversibly. In other words, a hydrogen-oxygen cell that produces water as a product can be made to regenerate hydrogen and oxygen. Such a regenerative fuel cell entails not only a revision of electrode design but also the introduction of special means for separating the product gases. Eventually, power modules comprising this type of high-efficiency fuel cell, used in conjunction with large arrays of thermal collectors for solar heating or other solar energy systems, may be utilized to keep energy-cycle costs lower in longer-lived equipment. Major automobile companies and electrical-machinery manufacturing companies worldwide have announced their intention to produce or use fuel cells commercially in the next few years.

DESIGNING FUEL CELL SYSTEMS

Because a fuel cell produces electricity continuously from fuel, it has many output characteristics similar to those of any other direct-current (DC) generator system. A DC generator system can be operated in either of two ways from a planning viewpoint: (1) fuel may be burned in a heat engine to drive an electric generator, which makes power available and current flow, or (2) fuel may be converted to a form suitable for a fuel cell, which then generates power directly.

A wide range of liquid and solid fuels may be used for a heat-engine system, while hydrogen, reformed natural gas (i.e., methane that has been converted to hydrogen-rich gas), and methanol are the primary fuels available for current fuel cells. If fuels such as natural gas must be altered in

A scientist examines prototypes of solid oxide fuel cells. Peter Ginter/Science Faction/Getty Images

composition for a fuel cell, the net efficiency of the fuel cell system is reduced, and much of its efficiency advantage is lost. Such an "indirect" fuel cell system would still display an efficiency advantage as high as 20 percent. Nonetheless, to be competitive with modern thermal generating plants, a fuel cell system must attain a good design balance with low internal electrical losses, corrosion-resistant electrodes, an electrolyte of constant composition, low catalyst costs, and ecologically acceptable fuels.

The first technical challenge that must be overcome in developing practical fuel cells is to design and assemble an electrode that allows the gaseous or liquid fuel to contact a catalyst and an electrolyte at a group of solid sites that do not change very rapidly. Thus, a three-phase reaction situation is typical on an electrode that must also serve as an electrical conductor. Such can be provided by thin sheets that have (1) a waterproof layer usually with polytetrafluoroethylene (Teflon), (2) an active layer of a catalyst (e.g., platinum, gold, or a complex organometallic compound on a carbon base), and (3) a conducting layer to carry the current generated in or out of the electrode. If the electrode floods with electrolyte, the operation rate will become very slow at best. If the fuel breaks through to the electrolyte side of the electrode, the electrolyte compartment may become filled with gas or vapour, inviting an explosion should the oxidizing gas also reach the electrolyte compartment or the fuel gas enter the oxidizing gas compartment. In short, to maintain stable operation in a working fuel cell, careful design, construction, and pressure control are essential. Because fuel cells have been used on Apollo lunar flights as well as on all other U.S. orbital manned space missions (e.g., those of Gemini and the space shuttle), it is evident that all three requirements can be met reliably.

Providing a fuel cell support system of pumps, blowers, sensors, and controls for maintaining fuel rates, electric current load, gas and liquid pressures, and fuel cell temperature remains a major engineering design challenge. Significant improvements in the service life of these components under adverse conditions would contribute to the wider use of fuel cells.

TYPES OF FUEL CELLS

Various types of fuel cells have been developed. They are generally classified on the basis of the electrolyte used, because the electrolyte determines the operating temperature of a system and in part the kind of fuel that can be employed.

ALKALINE FUEL CELLS

These are devices that, by definition, have an aqueous solution of sodium hydroxide or potassium hydroxide as the electrolyte. The fuel is almost always hydrogen gas, with oxygen (or oxygen in air) as the oxidizer. However, zinc or aluminum could be used as an anode if the by-product oxides were efficiently removed and the metal fed continuously as a strip or as a powder. Fuel cells generally operate at less than 100 °C (212 °F) and are constructed of metal and certain plastics. Electrodes are made of carbon and a metal such as nickel. Water, as a reaction product, must be removed from the system, usually by evaporation from the electrolyte either through the electrodes or in a separate evaporator.

The operating support system presents a significant design problem. The strong, hot alkaline electrolyte attacks most plastics and tends to penetrate structural seams and joints. This problem has been overcome, however, and alkaline fuel cells are used on the U.S. space shuttle orbiters. Overall efficiencies range from 30 to 80 percent, depending on the fuel and oxidizer and on the basis for the calculation.

PHOSPHORIC ACID FUEL CELLS

Phosphoric acid fuel cells have an orthophosphoric acid electrolyte that allows operation up to about 200 °C (400 °F). They can use a hydrogen fuel contaminated with carbon dioxide and an oxidizer of air or oxygen. The electrodes consist of catalyzed carbon and are arranged in pairs set back-to-back to create a series generation circuit. The framing structure for this assembly of cells is made of graphite, which markedly raises the cost. The higher temperature and aggressive hot phosphate create structural design problems, particularly for joints, supporting pumps, and sensors. Phosphoric acid fuel cells have been proposed and tested on a limited scale for local municipal power stations and for remote-site generators.

MOLTEN CARBONATE FUEL CELLS

Fuel cells of this type operate quite differently from those so far discussed. The fuel consists of a mixture of hydrogen and carbon monoxide generated from water and a fossil fuel. The electrolyte is molten potassium lithium carbonate, which requires an operating temperature of about 650 °C (1,200 °F). Warming up to operational temperatures may take several hours, making these cells unsuitable for vehicles. In most cases, the electrodes are metallic-based, and the containment system is made of metals and special engineering plastics. Such combinations of materials are anticipated to be relatively inexpensive, perhaps only three times that of the alkaline fuel cell and less than that of the phosphoric acid variety. The cells combine the hydrogen and carbon monoxide first with the carbonate electrolyte and then with oxidizing oxygen to produce a reaction product of water vapour and carbon dioxide.

Molten carbonate fuel cells are expected to be useful in both local and larger power stations. Efficiencies of 45 percent may be attained where fossil fuels are already used. Operation at high temperatures creates a design problem for long-lived system parts and joints, especially if the cells must be heated and cooled frequently. The toxic fuel and high temperature together make power plant safety an area of special concern in engineering design and testing as well as in commercial operation.

Solid Oxide Fuel Cells

In some ways solid oxide fuel cells are similar to molten carbonate devices. Most of the cell materials, however, are special ceramics with some nickel. The electrolyte is an ion-conducting oxide such as zirconia treated with yttria. The fuel for these experimental cells is expected to be hydrogen combined with carbon monoxide, just as for molten carbonate cells. While internal reactions would be different in terms of path, the cell products would be water vapour and carbon dioxide. Because of the high operating temperatures (900 to 1,000 °C, or 1,600 to 1,800 °F), the electrode reactions proceed very readily. As in the case of the molten carbonate fuel cell, there are many engineering challenges involved in creating a long-lived containment system for cells that operate at such a high-temperature range.

Solid oxide fuel cells would be designed for use in central power-generation stations where temperature variation could be controlled efficiently and where fossil fuels would be available. The system would in most cases be associated with the so-called bottoming steam (turbine) cycle—i.e., the hot gas product (at 1,000 °C [1,800 °F]) of the fuel cell could be used to generate steam to run a turbine and extract more power from heat energy. Overall efficiencies of 60 percent might be possible.

SOLID POLYMER ELECTROLYTE FUEL CELLS

A cell of this sort is built around an ion-conducting membrane such as Nafion (trademark for a perfluorosulfonic acid membrane). The electrodes are catalyzed carbon, and several construction alignments are feasible. Solid polymer electrolyte cells function well (as attested to by their performance in Gemini spacecraft), but cost estimates are high for the total system compared with the types described above. Engineering or electrode design improvements could change this disadvantage.

PROTON EXCHANGE MEMBRANE (PEM) FUEL CELL

The proton exchange membrane is one of the most advanced fuel cell designs. Hydrogen gas under pressure is forced through a catalyst, typically made of platinum, on the anode (negative) side of the fuel cell. At this catalyst, electrons are stripped from the hydrogen atoms and carried by an external electric circuit to the cathode (positive) side. The positively charged hydrogen ions (protons) then pass through the proton exchange membrane to the catalyst on the cathode side, where they react with oxygen and the electrons from the electric circuit to form water vapour (H_2O) and heat. The electric circuit is used to do work, such as power a motor.

DEVELOPMENT OF FUEL CELLS

The general concept of a fuel battery, or fuel cell, dates back to the early days of electrochemistry. British

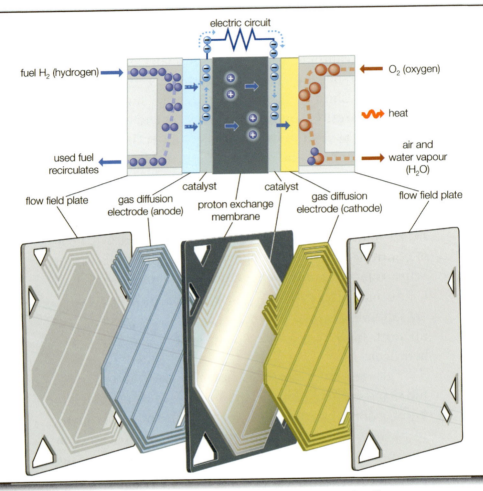

electric circuit

fuel H$_2$ (hydrogen)

O$_2$ (oxygen)

heat

air and
water vapour
(H$_2$O)

used fuel
recirculates

flow field plate

gas diffusion
electrode (anode)

catalyst

proton exchange
membrane

catalyst

gas diffusion
electrode (cathode)

flow field plate

Proton exchange membrane fuel cell. Encyclopædia Britannica, Inc.

physicist William Grove used hydrogen and oxygen as
fuels catalyzed on platinum electrodes in 1839. During
the late 1880s two British chemists—Carl Langer and
German-born Ludwig Mond—developed a fuel cell with
a longer service life by employing a porous nonconductor
to hold the electrolyte. It was subsequently found that a
carbon base permitted the use of much less platinum, and
the German chemist Wilhelm Ostwald proposed, as a sub-
stitute for heat-engine generators, electrochemical cells

in which carbon would be oxidized to carbon dioxide by oxygen. During the early years of the 20th century, Fritz Haber and Walther H. Nernst in Germany and Edmond Bauer in France experimented with cells using a solid electrolyte. Limited success and high costs, however, suppressed interest in continuing developmental efforts.

From 1932 until well after World War II, British engineer Francis Thomas Bacon and his coworkers at the University of Cambridge worked on creating practical hydrogen-oxygen fuel cells with an alkaline electrolyte. Research resulted in the invention of gas-diffusion electrodes in which the fuel gas on one side is effectively kept in controlled contact with an aqueous electrolyte on the other side. By mid-century O.K. Davtyan of the Soviet Union had published the results of experimental work on solid electrolytes for high-temperature fuel cells and for both high- and low-temperature alkaline electrolyte hydrogen-oxygen cells.

The need for highly efficient and stable power supplies for space satellites and manned spacecraft created exciting new opportunities for fuel cell development during the 1950s and '60s. Molten carbonate cells with magnesium oxide pressed against the electrodes were demonstrated by J.A.A. Ketelaar and G.H.J. Broers of the Netherlands, while the very thin Teflon-bonded, carbon-metal hybrid electrode was devised by other researchers. Many other technological advances, including the development of new materials, played a crucial role in the emergence of today's practical fuel cells.

Further improvements in electrode materials and construction, combined with the rising costs of fossil fuels, are expected to make fuel cells an increasingly attractive alternative power source, especially in Japan and other countries that have meagre nonrenewable energy resources. At the beginning of the 21st century, many electrical-equipment manufacturers were developing power-generation equipment based on fuel cell technology. The American military is funding development of small fuel cells for soldiers to carry in their backpacks in order to power various electronic devices, for powering small pilotless reconnaissance aircraft, and for powering robots to clear minefields.

CONCLUSION

Growing concern over the world's ever-increasing energy needs and the prospect of dwindling reserves of oil and natural gas have prompted efforts to develop viable alternative energy sources. The volatility and uncertainty of the petroleum fuel supply were dramatically brought to the fore during the energy crisis of the 1970s, caused by the abrupt curtailment of oil shipments from the Middle East to many of the highly industrialized nations of the world. It also has been recognized that the heavy reliance on fossil fuels has had an adverse impact on the environment. Gasoline engines and steam-turbine power plants that burn coal or natural gas emit substantial amounts of sulfur dioxide and nitrogen oxides into the atmosphere, where they give rise to highly acidic precipitation. The combustion of fossil fuels also releases carbon dioxide into the atmosphere, which most environmental scientists have concluded contributes to a greenhouse effect that raises the surface temperature of the Earth.

Many countries have initiated programs to develop alternative energy technologies that would enable them to reduce fossil-fuel consumption and its attendant problems. Since the mid-20th century, the most prominent alternative to fossil fuels has been nuclear energy, making use of the abundant energy locked within the atomic nucleus to produce electric power. Nuclear power is still an important alternative, but it is a controversial one, owing to the possibility of catastrophic accidents and to the fact that the nuclear-power programs of many countries have been linked to the development of nuclear weapons.

Other technologies that are being actively pursued are those designed to make wider and more efficient use of the energy in sunlight, wind, moving water, and terrestrial heat (i.e., geothermal energy). The amount of energy in such renewable and virtually pollution-free sources is large in relation to world energy needs, yet at the present time only a small portion of it can be converted to electric power at reasonable cost.

A variety of devices and systems has been created to better tap the energy in sunlight. Among the most efficient are photovoltaic systems that transform radiant energy from the Sun directly into electricity by means of silicon or gallium arsenide solar cells. Large arrays consisting of thousands of these semiconductor cells have been built to function as central power stations. Other systems are designed to concentrate solar radiation not only to generate electric power but also to produce high-temperature process heat for various applications. These systems employ a number of different components, including large parabolic concentrators and flat-plate solar collectors to provide space heating for commercial and residential buildings.

Although wind is intermittent and diffuse, it contains tremendous amounts of energy. Sophisticated wind turbines have been developed to convert this energy to electric power, and hundreds of individual wind turbines have been linked together in vast wind farms to serve as major power installations.

Converting the energy in moving water to electricity is a long-standing technology used in hydroelectric power plants. The technology involved is simple enough: water turbines change the energy of fast-flowing or falling water into mechanical energy that drives power generators, which produce electricity. Hydroelectric power plants, however, generally require the building of costly dams. Another factor that limits any significant increase in hydroelectric power production is the scarcity of suitable sites for additional installations except in certain regions of the world.

In certain coastal areas of the world, as, for example, the Rance River estuary in Brittany, France, hydraulic turbine-generator units have been used to harness the great amount of energy in ocean tides. At other sites, turbines have been installed to tap the power of tidal currents and the up-and-down motion of ocean waves.

Geothermal energy flows from the hot interior of the Earth to the surface in steam or hot water most often in areas of active volcanism. Geothermal reservoirs with temperatures of 180 °C (356 °F) or higher are suitable for power generation. The earliest commercial geothermal power plant was built in 1904 in Larderello, Italy. Today, steam from wells drilled to depths of hundreds of metres still drives the plant's turbine generators. Geothermal plants have been built in a number of other countries, including El Salvador, Japan, Mexico, New Zealand, and the United States.

As a possible alternative to gasoline-powered automobiles or coal-fired power plants, fuel cells have been proposed and many prototypes built. The devices are efficient at generating electricity directly from chemical reactions, but they are expensive to fabricate, and the fuel used to supply the reaction, usually hydrogen or methane, is itself derived from fossil fuels or is obtained from energy-intensive processes. At this time fuel cells are employed most profitably as reliable long-lived power sources for spacecraft and other isolated vehicles.

biomass The total quantity of organic matter, including all the plants and animal species, in an area at a certain moment.

cellulose A major carbohydrate found in the cell walls of plants, as well as in some algae and fungi.

cladding A material that covers or overlays; specifically, a substance that isolates nuclear fuel from the coolant and keeps radioactive fission products contained.

criticality The steady rate of nuclear fission that is reached when an average of one neutron from a fission causes another fission.

enthalpy Amount of heat energy a substance possesses, measurable in terms of the heat change that accompanies a chemical reaction carried out at constant pressure.

estuary A water passage where the tide meets a river current.

ethanol A colourless liquid alcohol that is the active constituent of alcoholic drinks but is also used for industrial purposes and as a fuel.

fission The splitting of an atom's nucleus into parts with similar masses in order to release energy.

fusion The reaction between light atomic nuclei in which a heavier nucleus is formed, thus producing energy.

geothermal energy Refers to power obtained using heat from Earth's interior.

penstock A conduit for conducting the flow of water.

photovoltaic Used to describe the process in which two dissimilar materials in close contact produce an electrical voltage when struck by light or other radiant energy.

quern An ancient device used for grinding grain.

rotor An assembly of rotating blades, the central shaft of which is coupled to a mechanical prime mover.

semiconductor A crystalline solid that is intermediate in electrical conductivity between a conductor and an insulator.

sluice An artificial passage for water (as in a mill-stream) fitted with a valve or gate for stopping or regulating flow.

terawatt hour A unit of measurement for large amount of energy, roughly the equivalent of 1 million kilowatt hours.

tidal barrage A system that takes advantage of differences between high and low tides that uses a dam to block receding water during ebb periods.

turbine A device that passes flowing water, steam, or the wind through a system of fixed and moving fanlike blades, causing them to rotate and create mechanical energy.

wicket gate A mechanical device that alters the flow of kinetic energy.

BIBLIOGRAPHY

Hermann Scheer, *The Solar Economy: Renewable Energy for a Sustainable Global Future* (2002), by an internationally known advocate for renewable energy, argues that solar power is an economically viable alternative to fossil fuels. Joel Davidson and Fran Orner, *The New Solar Electric Home: The Complete Guide to Photovoltaics for Your Home*, 3rd ed. (2008), is a practical handbook accessible to a non-technically trained reader. Richard J. Komp, *Practical Photovoltaics: Electricity from Solar Cells*, 3rd ed. rev. (2001), is more advanced but still accessible and contains much practical information. Stephen J. Fonash, *Solar Cell Device Physics*, 2nd ed. (2010), is for device specialists; and Roger A. Messenger and Jerry Ventre, *Photovoltaic Systems Engineering*, 2nd ed. (2004), is for systems and applications specialists.

Paul Gipe, *Wind Power: Renewable Energy for Home, Farm, and Business*, revised and expanded ed. (2003), is an illustrated and comprehensive book on all practical aspects of choosing and installing wind systems. Another comprehensive book at a more advanced level is Tony Burton et al., *Wind Energy Handbook* (2001).

Roger Henri Charlier and Charles W. Finkl, *Ocean Energy: Tide and Tidal Power* (2009), surveys all methods for generating power from the sea, from tides and waves to thermal and saline gradients. David Ross, *Power From the Waves* (1995), analyzes the science and also the politics of wave power, with particular reference to the United Kingdom.

Two books on geothermal energy for students and professionals are Mary H. Dickson and Mario Fanelli (eds.), *Geothermal Energy: Utilization and Technology* (2005); and Ronald DiPippo, *Geothermal Power Plants: Principles, Applications, Case Studies, and Environmental Impact*, 2nd ed. (2008).

Worldwatch Institute, *Biofuels for Transport: Global Potential and Implications for Sustainable Energy and Agriculture* (2007), includes sections on current and emerging technologies, economic and social issues, environmental issues, and policy recommendations. International Energy Agency, *Biofuels for Transport: An International Perspective* (2004), is an economic assessment that considers environmental costs and benefits and compares production and delivery costs of biofuels relative to other fuels.

Raymond L. Murray, *Nuclear Energy: An Introduction to the Concepts, Systems, and Application of Nuclear Processes*, 6th ed. (2009), is a popular textbook covering reactor concepts, radiation, nuclear fuel cycles, reactor systems, and safety and safeguards. The same topics are covered at more advanced levels in Ronald Allen Knief, *Nuclear Engineering: Theory and Technology of Commercial Nuclear Power*, 2nd ed. (2008); and John R. Lamarsh and Anthony John Baratta, *Introduction to Nuclear Engineering*, 3rd ed. (2001). Current developments in domestic and international nuclear power, safety, research, and opinion are published in *Nuclear News* (monthly), the newsletter of the American Nuclear Society.

General references on fuel cells include James Larminie and Andrew Dicks, *Fuel Cell Systems Explained*, 2nd ed. (2003); Gregor Hoogers (ed.), *Fuel Cell Technology Handbook* (2003); and Wolf Vielstich, Arnold Lamm, and Hubert A. Gasteiger (eds.), *Handbook of Fuel Cells: Fundamentals, Technology, Applications*, 4 vol. (2003).

INDEX